THE ART OF PSYCHIC PROTECTION

Judy Hall

D1259719

WEISER BOOKS

Boston, MA/York Beach, ME

First published in 1997 by
Red Wheel/Weiser, LLC
368 Congress Street
Boston, MA 02210
www.redwheelweiser.com

Library of Congress Cataloging-in-Publication Data

Hall, Judy.
        The art of psychic protection / Judy Hall.
            p.   cm.
        Originally published: Forres, Scotland : Findhorn Press, 1996
        Includes index.
        ISBN 1-57863-026-6 (pbk. : alk. paper)
        1. Self-defense—Psychic aspects. I. Title.
BF1045.S46H35   1997   97-11035
133—dc21   CIP

VG
Typeset in Goudy Old Style

Cover illustration is "Sobek in the Guise of Protector God," copyright © 1997
Judith Page / Artists Rights Society (ARS), New York / DACS, London.
"Sekhmet" on page 37 is a photograph of a painting copyright © 1997 Judith Page
/ Artists Rights Society (ARS), New York / DACS, London. Used by permission.

Printed in the United States of America

08 07 06 05 04
10 9   8   7   6   5   4

The paper used in this publication meets the minimum requirements of the
American National Standard for Information Sciences—Permanence of Paper for
Printed Library Materials Z39.48-1992(R1997).

❧ Contents ❧

❧ Acknowledgments ❧

I OWE AN ENORMOUS DEBT OF GRATITUDE to the late Christine Hartley who was much more than a mentor to me. In her twilight years, long after she thought such work was over, she took a novice and created a competent what-can-I-call-it? Psychic, healer, regression therapist, walker of esoteric paths. All of these are true and yet with Christine's help, the whole is greater than its parts. I owe a large part of what I have become to her loving friendship and unending care.

I would also like to thank Thelma Reardon who taught me many things, and will no doubt recognize some of her techniques.

I am indebted to the three people who taught me most about psychic attack and gave me an opportunity to put theory into practice in a big way. It might have been hell, but I would not have missed it for the world! I do not need to name them, they know who they are. Thank you!

My thanks to everyone from whom I have learned along the way, intentionally or not, especially Dave Gilbert, and to all those who have made this book possible.

And finally, to my partner Robert Jacobs who patiently read the manuscript, offered perceptive comments and informed criticism, added in his own wisdom and, most importantly, took me to Egypt, my love and thanks as always.

❧ Warning

It has been brought to my attention that people might be tempted to misuse some of the techniques and information in this book in order to perpetrate psychic attack.

vi ❧ THE ART OF PSYCHIC PROTECTION

I cannot stress too strongly how unwise this would be. Such a course of action would inevitably rebound back onto the perpetrator.

Please use this book for your own protection.

Judy Hall

❧ Introduction ❧

❧ Why Do We Need Psychic Protection?

Humankind excels at protection. We protect ourselves against the elements: we wear clothes and build houses. We protect ourselves against other people: we lock our doors and build walls. We put our money into banks, our future into pension funds. We squander millions on arms that are intended to protect us against "the enemy," someone *other*. We can insure ourselves against virtually every eventuality. And yet, few people even realize that there is a much more subtle intrusion against which bolts and bars are powerless, for which the only insurance is to be aware, and where we often find that we are our own greatest enemy.

- *Do you meditate, seek to expand your consciousness, do path-work, set out on shamanic journeys, take drugs?*
- *Are you a therapist or healer?*
- *Do you use guided imagery or self-hypnosis tapes?*
- *Do you find people naturally gravitate to you with their troubles?*
- *Are you perpetually tired, listless, overcome by inexplicable emotion or hopelessness, with an indefinable sense of invasion or wrongness?*
- *Do you suffer from nightmares?*
- *Are you suddenly accident-prone, nothing working in your life?*
- *Has anyone ever, deliberately or inadvertently, placed you under psychic attack?*

If so, the chances are you need psychic protection.

Psychic has two meanings. One pertains to things of the psyche: that inner part of us which encompasses not only our conscious mind and convictions, but also the subconscious mind and the irrational beliefs associated with it. The other meaning pertains to the unseen, hidden, esoteric and occult part of our being that exists beyond the purely physical. This is the realm of non-verbal communication, telepathy, subtle energy bodies, other dimensions of consciousness, and the different levels of being. Psychic protection is relevant to both these meanings, as we shall see.

Psychic protection is subtle and invisible. It works on a non-physical level of being, although it is inextricably linked with the body. It resonates to the principle of "like attracts like." It teaches us the true power of thought. It surrounds us with a protective barrier within which we can safely expand our spiritual perception, or go about our daily life. At its simplest level, psychic protection can be a hoop of light around your feet, which you pull up all around you when required. It can be a bubble you inhabit, a crystal you keep around yourself. The key is to find exactly the right method for you, and for the situations you find yourself in. As psychic protection works on an invisible, vibrational level, it can be enhanced by using the subtle energy fields of flower essences and crystals. Where appropriate, I have included the relevant essences in the text and there is a section devoted to their use and properties. Above all else though, psychic protection is about being fully grounded in your body. If you only have a toehold on the earth, you will never be fully secure.

The explosion of consciousness that has taken place over the last few years has had powerful effects. Esoteric knowledge that had been kept hidden for eternity and only revealed to carefully chosen, and meticulously prepared, initiates is now available to anyone with the money to purchase the book or attend the workshop. Techniques are peddled, mysteries sold. Talismans are offered to attract luck, or divert ill-fortune. The

Internet even carries a banishing ritual in case you are being haunted by Elvis Presley. The occult is a subject that magnetically attracts the weird and the bizarre and, therefore, puts people off. But, whenever you meditate, you are using an occult method. Whenever you mentally ask for a taxi to come along, you are invoking: another occult technique. Occult simply means hidden knowledge. Magic is manipulating unseen forces to influence events, objects or people. This is knowledge that is coming into the open fast and furiously.

However, it is all too easy to meddle with things you do not really understand and cannot control, to pick up negative energies from people or places because you are too open. Expanding our consciousness takes us into unknown realms, realms where we may meet more than we bargained for. It also opens up our chakras, the subtle energy centers of the body. If we do not remember to close these down again, it leaves us wide open. We are like a beacon shining out who knows where, to attract whatever is out there. We can become a psychic vacuum cleaner to all that is around us. Unfortunately it is also, as I am uncomfortably reminded from time to time, possible to antagonize someone who has powerful energies and who, consciously or unconsciously, directs these energies into attack mode. Opening up our consciousness makes us much more sensitive, and susceptible, to "bad vibes." Few introductory texts and courses on meditation, consciousness-raising or complementary therapies pay attention to the essential art of psychic protection.

- If you have found yourself feeling tired, edgy, "out of sort," inexplicably depressed or oppressed,
- If you feel that there are "entities" around you that wish you harm,
- If your life is somehow going wrong, nothing you touch comes right, small accidents keep happening, "something" is thwarting you,
- If you feel out of control, ungrounded and invaded,

then, you are keeping company with the many people who contact me asking for help. They have all learned to open up, but not to close down again. They are giving too much to their clients and patients, and not taking enough time for themselves. They are suffering from energy drainage, or from adverse environmental energies (geopathic stress). Sometimes they have had the misfortune, or the audacity, to attract the malice, or envy, of someone else. They are being psychically attacked. Even when we know about psychic protection and the need to cleanse our energies, we forget. As one healer put it, "I must remember to make each breath a cleansing and protection for me."

We must also remember it is possible to inadvertently psychically attack someone else ourselves. Someone angers us. We argue. We go away still carrying on that argument in our head. We admonish, we rage, we curse. We may think, "I wish he or she were dead/hurt/punished." Our thoughts reach that person. Thought has energy and effects. This was shown to me all too clearly many years ago in the days before I understood just how powerful the mind is. I was in therapy and my teenage daughter was being the kind of problem all teenage daughters are from time to time. My therapist suggested I should use a gestalt technique to express exactly how angry I was. There, on a chair, I was to imagine my daughter. I ranted and raged, telling her how thoughtless and selfish she was. How I longed to shake her till her teeth rattled! I expended a great deal of psychic energy. And, when I went home, there was my daughter prostrate with migraine. As a healer I should have known that what can heal can also destroy. My thoughts and anger had reached her and she had no defense against it.

Prevention is better than cure. To wait until you need psychic protection, is too late. Everyone who opens up their awareness needs simple techniques for screening, closing and protection—now! Protection needs to be something you can do quickly and easily. It is no good selecting complicated rituals. Practicing daily, before you need it, means that you will be automatically protected if problems arise. You may also need to protect the space in which you work or meditate. All the techniques in this book are tried and tested; some date back thousands of years, others belong to the 21st century. All can be learned quickly and will soon become automatic.

I am well aware that there are other methods of protection, but I have chosen to write about the ones that I have personally worked with over the last twenty years. I know that what you will find in this book works. The object is to prevent intrusion or interference from any unwanted source. The aim is to cleanse and strengthen our own natural protective energies. There are times when it is appropriate to open up to someone else, to feel what they are feeling—maybe even to draw off negative energies, but this must be a conscious and considered choice. And, if we are to remain physically and psychologically healthy, we must know how to clear ourselves afterwards.

Many of the techniques in this book use visualization, the power of the mind to create images that are then translated into action on the subtle levels of being. If you don't "see" anything at first, "act as if"—that is, go through the exercise acting as though you can see. It will work on the inner levels. Intention gets transmuted into action. Inner experience is integrated into your state of being.

While the forming of images can improve with practice—and can be helped by looking up at the point above and between your eyebrows—a small percentage of people will never "see" anything. They are non-visual. If you are one of these people do not despair. You will have other abilities which can take over: the capacity to sense or feel, to hear an inner voice, to simply know. Once you have learned to trust this process, you can adapt the techniques accordingly. (I have given suggestions at the end of each exercise.) Even if you can see images, allowing yourself to feel or sense makes the experience much more powerful—and therefore that much more effective.

This book is divided into sections for easy reference. Some of the material inevitably overlaps between sections, which means it may appear in more than one place. I am not repeating myself just for the sake of it: I wanted the sections to be complete in themselves—as far as possible. You may still have to turn to another page to find the appropriate technique set out in detail. Just to be sure you can find the relevant exercise quickly, an index of visualizations is included (pages 134–142).

Some of the observations and techniques may seem obvious to you, others rather strange, some downright wrong. This may be due to the language used: it may explain things differently from what you have been used to. Or, it may be that you have never encountered such things before. I am aware that I now take for granted a great many things that make other people go "Whaa..t??," which is why this book arises out of my own experience not mere theory. I have encountered these things over many years. I know they exist. My aim is not to make you afraid. Fear destroys protection. I do, however, believe in being forewarned. You may be lucky, you may never come under psychic attack. You may never have an involuntary out-of-the-body experience that puts you in an unsafe place. You may never have to deal with an unwanted psychic communicator. But, if you do, you will know how to deal with it once you have read this book. So, if there are things that you cannot yet accept, or question the validity of, may I suggest you put them on a mental shelf, and every so often take them down, dust them off and see how they feel. What I do not suggest is that you use a technique, or take on a belief, that feels wrong to you. That is no protection at all.

As you work through this book, you will learn many techniques and be offered some valuable aids for protecting yourself, your space, those around you. But, before doing so, it is helpful to understand something of the aura and the different levels of our being.

❧ Natural Protection: The Aura ❧

HUMAN BEINGS ARE NOT SIMPLY PHYSICAL bodies defined by, and enclosed within, a barrier of skin. We have subtle energy bodies that extend out towards, and interact with, everything around us, including other people. Our thoughts and feelings reach others, just as their emotions wash over us. Sensitive people can pick up other people's physical or emotional conditions. Have you developed a headache, only to have the person sitting next to you complain of exactly the same pain? Sometimes we take that pain away with us without ever knowing it is not ours. We may feel drained and exhausted after a quick word with someone. A few desperate souls act like psychic leeches: vampires don't only exist in fiction! Similarly, we may feel down after meeting a particular person, or good after spending time with another, a feeling which has nothing to do with what has passed between us verbally. It is all a question of the energies they are giving out and how we respond.

It is not necessary to be in physical proximity for our energies to interact. We can communicate with other people over vast distances simply by thinking about them. How often have you found yourself wondering how so-and-so is, only to have them call a few moments later? All of these activities take place through the subtle energy bodies that comprise our aura. If our aura is strong, we will be well protected. However, shock and trauma can lead to "breaks," or weakness, in the auric field as can psychic attack and geopathic stress, such as electromagnetic radiation. Any weakness makes us more vulnerable to negative influences and psychic invasion.

Some people are able to see the aura that surrounds us. This is a multi-layered energy field that pulsates with color according to our mood and health. It resonates with the emotional, mental and spiritual levels of being. As auric photographs show, each person's aura is unique. In one person it may extend out several feet; in another it will be tight and close to the body. Angry reds and magentas may predominate, or pale blues and pinks: in the first instance they belong to fiery, strong-willed persons, often with great anger, while in the second case people will be much more passive and calm, and may be low in vitality. In meditation, the aura expands and becomes golden. Intuitives can usually "see" how we are feeling from the colors we are giving out. Gifted psychics are able to read in this aura our whole emotional history. Indeed for many it is like an auto-biography. All the details of our lives are set out there.

For most of us, this aura remains an unseen mystery, and yet it is our link to other people. We may unconsciously "read" auras to know what other people are thinking or feeling. Children especially tune into auras and may well include them in drawings of family or friends. I have a wonderful portrait by my, then, 3-year-old granddaughter. I am on tiptoe, with a huge yellow balloon around my head and shoulders. At the time I was engaged in writing a book. Yellow is the color of mental activity. As for being on tiptoe, well, even at the best of times I have to work hard to stay grounded. When I am writing, I am consciously reaching up for inspiration and my contact with the ground becomes even more tenuous. She saw exactly my state of being. When she drew her mother, there was a black balloon at the solar plexus. It was some time before it became apparent to the adults around her that her mother was seriously depressed. But the child had seen it.

Those who can see auras describe what happens when we interact with another person as: "the colors merging and mingling," "the energies becoming entangled," "tentacles reaching out," "a siphon sucking off energy from one person into the other." In healing or empathetic therapy, energy from the therapist will blend with the patient. In love, and especially in orgasm, the two auras will, for a time, become one. When our interaction is finished, we may each take away a small part of the other's energy field. Unless we are aware of this intermingling, we do not realize that we need to withdraw our energies and reestablish our boundary afterwards.

So, by becoming aware of the aura and strengthening its protective function, we can safeguard ourselves against unwanted intrusion or insidious energy leakage. A simple visualization exercise, performed twice a day for a few days, will vastly increase the amount of protection available from your aura. The exercise will become habitual, and can be used in emergency situations when you are aware of needing extra protection simply by thinking, "Light Bubble." You can also use the vibrationary healing of flower essences to cleanse and strengthen the aura. The Australian Bush Essence Fringed Violet is particularly good for repairing any weakness. Anyone who suffers from sensitivity to other people's emanations, and particularly therapists or practitioners, who interact with subtle energies all the time, will find the Gem Auric Protection Remedy most effective. (Other remedies are given in the section on Flower and Gem Essences.)

⸙ Using Guided Imagery

The power of the imagination is immense. Whatever we can image, we can bring into being. All the visualization exercises in this book utilize our "inner screen." This is positioned between, and slightly above, our eyebrows. It is the "third eye" chakra. If you have difficulty visualizing, looking up to this spot (without opening your eyes) helps the images to form. The Australian Bush Flower Essence, Boronia, which works on a vibration level attuned to the aura, can help with focusing creative visualization as well as quieting the mind in preparation for meditation—as can Bush Iris which opens up higher perceptions. If you find excessive thoughts are a problem, the Bach Flower Remedy White Chestnut helps to clear the mind chatter. Black Eyed Susan helps you to slow down, turn inward and find the calm center within. A few drops of the essences taken in water before beginning the exercises in this book, will prove helpful.

However, some people will never "see" anything during one of these exercises. They will discover other ways of doing things. Do not try to force images. Because we are invoking the power of thought, it can be helpful to "act as if"—that is to say, to do the exercise as though you are seeing something on that inner screen even when you are not. Gradually, you will develop the feeling, rather than the picture. Whether or not you see the images, it is this feeling of something happening that is important. When you can get a sense of the exercise working around you, of the bubble being there, then you will know that your protection is in place. As with all the exercises in this book, you can memorize it or tape it if you wish, allowing time to carry out all the instructions without hurrying. If you wish to, play a favorite piece of relaxation music in the background to aid you.

If you have difficulty in relaxing, raise and lower your eyelids ten times. On the tenth time, allow them to stay closed. Then let the feeling of relaxation in your eyelids flow down to your feet. Or, imagine yourself getting into an elevator which will take you down to the optimum level for relaxation. After a little practice, getting in the elevator and saying "basement" will automatically take you into deep relaxation.

❧ The Light Bubble

Close your eyes and breathe gently. Let yourself relax and soften, breathing out any tension you may be feeling and breathing in a sense of peace and relaxation. Take as long as you need to settle comfortably, gradually withdrawing your attention from the outside world and into yourself.

Look up to your inner screen. On that screen, project a pic- Bead *ture of a place where you feel happy and protected. It may be a grassy glade, a beach, a church, a garden, a place from your childhood. An actual place or one you imagine. Think about that place, and it will appear on the screen. Spend a few minutes enjoying that place, remembering how good it feels. Let your feet walk there, feeling the ground beneath them. Let your senses bring to you the smell of the place, its own unique, fragrant perfume. Let your skin tell you how warm it is.*

Gradually you will become aware that there is a shaft of bright light shining down and touching the ground in front of you. light *This light pulsates with energy and flashes of color. Indeed, it may be a special color which you need. Or it may be white, containing all the colors within it.*

Let yourself go into this light. Stand within it and absorb light into your whole being. Breathe it in, absorb it through your skin, and allow it to permeate your aura. Fill your aura with light and vitality. After a while, you will become conscious of your aura stretching out around you in vibrant color. See the different colored layers flowing out around your body. Check your aura's level of vitality; if you need more, breathe in more light. If it is overpoweringly strong, let it find its appropriate level.

Notice how far out your aura extends. Feel its edges. You can use your physical hands to reach out and touch the edge, or mentally reach out all around you probing its limits. You will find that it is roughly egg-shaped. It extends over your head and below your feet. Check whether it has any breaks or weaknesses. You can experiment with this aura: pull it in close to you, allow it to widen out again. Let it settle, ending at an appropriate distance from your physical body. Knowing the boundary of your aura protects you, so spend as long as you need to become familiar with it.

If you feel you need extra protection, you can "crystallize"' your aura's outer edge, making it strong and hard but translucent so you can see out. You will be encased in an egg-shaped crystal full of light.

When you are ready, step out from the column of light. Check that your aura is still glowing, full of light. Check that its boundary is strong and intact. It should completely surround you, forming an impenetrable protective barrier around you. This is your cloak of protection. Nothing can impinge through the aura unless you choose to allow it in. Nothing can drain its energy and vitality. You are protected.

When you are ready, gently bring your awareness back into the room. Be aware of your physical body, of your feet on the earth. Breathe a little more deeply. Move your hands and feet. Get up and stretch. Be aware too of your aura and its protective function. From now on, you will live within a bubble of light.

If you are non-visual: *Physically* feel your aura with your hands—with a little practice you will feel a warm tingling at the outer edges. Any breaks or weaknesses will be felt as cold spots. Pull it out with your hands, push it in. Find the most comfortable distance. When you know how far it stretches, sense the white light surrounding it, feel its warmth and brightness, and continue the exercise from there.

❧ The Cloak of Protection

When you are deeply relaxed, picture yourself walking into a column of light (in whatever color feels right for you). Wrap this light around your aura so that it forms a cloak of protection. Let it cover your head and sweep right down to your feet. When you are wearing this cloak, nothing can intrude or impress itself on you. You can wrap the cloak around yourself, which will give you complete protection, or open it if you want your psychic energies to interact with someone else. Whenever you finish meditation, or any other psychic or spiritual opening up, ensure that the cloak is wrapped firmly around yourself.

If you are non-visual, or for extra protection during meditation and other psychic work, you may like to make a suitable cloak to wear.

❧ The Grounding Cord

Picture a cord running from the bottom of your feet deep down into the earth. This cord holds you in incarnation. It is flexible, it allows you to move, but it is hooked into the center of the Earth anchoring your physical body in everyday reality. With this cord in place, you will always be grounded and earthed.

⟩ Levels of Being ⟨

THE AURA HAS A PHYSICAL, EMOTIONAL, mental and spiritual or causal component. It is formed of layers which vibrate at different frequencies. These layers have a complex interaction and there are various schools of thought as to how many layers exist, and in what order. All you need to know in order to protect yourself is that all of life operates at these different levels of vibration, and it is possible to interact with these frequencies at more than one level. You can enhance the integrated functioning of the different levels by the use of an agate crystal, which helps to harmonize the mind, body and spirit.

The diagram on the next page is a simplified, one-dimensional version and should not be taken too literally:

The base level of being is the physical. This is where matter vibrates at its most dense frequency and, therefore, appears most solid. It is the level of form. Although, of course, physicists tell us that, in reality, even an apparently "solid" body contains huge empty spaces where solar winds blow. At the physical level of being we need our senses to interact with the world. We cannot share our physical space with another human being, unless of course we are pregnant and, even then, the fetus is contained with its own skin and aura, cushioned in its own watery world.

Sight, hearing, touch, smell and taste are our tools for exploring what is around us. At this level, we communicate with words or pictorial representations. What we can see is real, what we can touch is tangible, what we can taste exists. Even so, we may be aware that there are unseen forces, such as radio- or micro-waves passing through the ether around us.

Higher consciousness

Casual level/spiritual realms

Beyond death

"Peak experiences"

Deep meditation

Thought forms
Telepathy
Channeling
Out-of-Body experiences
Extra-Sensory perception
Psychic experiences

Sense perception

Physical, mental and
emotional experiences

Spiritual

Mental

Emotional

Physical

Edge of aura

The subconscious
The collective unconscious

Spiritual realms

Higher astral

Lower astral

Physical plane

The aura and levels of being.

When people see auras, it is often the "physical" level they see. It shows itself as a brightish, white or gray glow close to the body. This is sometimes known as the etheric or astral body. If part of the body is cut away, the aura still retains the full outline of the missing part. This aura shows our state of physical health: ease or dis-ease.

At the emotional level of being, matter vibrates in a different way. It is resonating at a higher frequency. Our emotional body occupies the same space as the physical, but also extends beyond it. Yes, we experience feelings and emotions in various parts of our bodies, fear catches in our gut, our heart lifts with joy or sinks with sorrow. But our experience is also beyond the physical. When we hug someone, the act is physical, but the feelings that pass between us come through our emotional body. If we are intuitive and empathetic, we can genuinely share what others are feeling because some of their "emotional matter" is transferred to us. If we are not, then we rely on our intellectual understanding of what that feeling is, of our own memories of a time when we felt like that, to know how they feel. Communication at this level of being does not need words, although it may include them. It often comes through touch or smell. (Fear has a raw, rancid odor all of its own.)

If we are pregnant, the fetus shares what we feel; our blood carries with it the tang of fear, the sweetness of joy. Chemical couriers cross the placenta carrying our emotional messages. But the baby can also intuit much of what we are feeling. Contrary to popular opinion, the child in the womb is conscious and aware. If it is wanted, it feels warm and welcomed. If it is not, it feels cold and rejected. This is relevant to psychic protection because sometimes we are sensitized to extremes of emotion before birth. Some children cannot keep their mother's strong feelings out, others learn to shut off very quickly. We continue to operate these early patterns as we mature. Someone with the first pattern is vulnerable to emotional invasion. Someone with the second is more susceptible to mental interference. But both are open to psychic intrusion.

This emotional level of being has its counterpart in the aura, interpenetrating to other layers. It is not, however, available to "normal" sight. It needs a psychic eye. It is said that once out of the physical body, we cannot hide our emotions as then this aura is visible to everyone. So, Earth is the place where we conceal our emotions, play emotional games, wreak emotional havoc on ourselves and others. And so, this is one of the levels most vulnerable to psychic attack.

At the mental level, our being vibrates faster. Our mental body reaches out to others in its desire to communicate and to understand. When we share thoughts, when we are fired with enthusiasm, our "mental stuff" flows out in great waves. We communicate at this level through ideas, symbols, metaphors and stories, conveying subtle nuances of meaning. It is at this level that the "sixth-sense" operates. Extra-sensory perception does not rely on physical communication, can cross space and time, and is often beyond our conscious control. Telepathy, reception of another's thought across space without words or visual communication, worked on the first Moon Mission. Images were sent from the Moon, and received on Earth, purely by thought transmission. The power of thought is immense. It can affect our health, our wealth, what we attract and what we repel. It can influence others, start great movements, destroy civilizations. Whatever we can imagine, or image, we can bring into being through controlled thought power. An awesome thought indeed, and one which makes us take responsibility for every thought we have, once we realize how our thoughts affect others.

Extra-sensory perception is particularly strong between mother and child. Regressed back to the womb, many people know instinctively what their mother, and other family members, are thinking as well as feeling. In most of us, this faculty shuts down soon after birth. However, in some people it continues and can cause confusion between what the child is told by others, and what he or she receives as intuitive impressions. Most people either shut down the ESP, or retreat into their own inner world and distrust what they are told by others. If the ESP is still going full blast, then the child acts like a radar screen, picking up everything around them. Unless they develop a strong boundary between themselves and the outside world, they act like a psychic sponge, soaking up other people's thoughts and feelings. Such a child may need to learn psychic protection at a very early age, as otherwise they can be easily overwhelmed. Schizophrenia is just one mental dis-ease that can arise from the inability to screen out other peoples' "stuff."

The aura for the mental body acts as a vehicle for psychic impressions to be conveyed. It also acts as a go-between for the spiritual, emotional and physical levels of being, helping them to communicate and process insights, feelings and intuitions. In people who are intellectually orientated, the mental aura is expanded and highly charged. In those who are overly emotional, the mental aura is compressed and tight.

People tend to operate through either the emotional body or the mental body. The mental body is cerebral, the emotional body is intuitive. This leads to either an analytical, intellectual approach to life, or an illogical, feeling orientation. Neither is better than the other. They are simply different ways of looking at the world. But, the latter is more susceptible to outside influences.

Then, we have the spiritual/causal level of being. This is where the eternal, spiritual self resides. The part that is vibrating at the highest, most ethereal level possible on the material plane. To get fully into the spiritual body is the goal of enlightenment seekers everywhere. To stay consciously at this level is difficult, most of us can only touch it for moments at a time although this is something we can improve with practice. But, once we are in our spiritual body, then we are in touch with universal consciousness, with the cosmos, god, bliss, call it what you will. This is where we know without question that we are divine beings and that we do have a higher purpose. It is where we can reach out to a source of love that never fails, to an energy that enfolds us in a protective parent-like embrace and yet gives us absolute freedom to be what we must be. It is where we can receive help and guidance, spiritual companionship, and joy.

The spiritual aura is the halo of saints. They had developed their connection with the spiritual body until it was visible to all, or at least to those with the eyes to see. Our own spiritual auras may need a little work, some polishing, but they are always there. If our spiritual aura is strong, then we have natural protection.

This is the highest level able to connect to the earth plane. Beyond this, the levels of being are non-material. The astral or etheric is where the soul passes to after death, and from which some "lost" souls may reach back to the Earth for comfort, or revenge. There are higher planes beyond through which we must all evolve, but we are not concerned with these here except to note that we can interpenetrate these levels beyond the earth plane in states of expanded consciousness, or when we are psychically "stuck open."

The astral levels—lower and higher—are where souls travel after death. Most of the communication from "the other side" comes from these levels of vibration: usually from souls who are stuck there and have not passed onto the higher spiritual realms. It is also possible to pass to these levels during an out-of-body experience when our astral, or etheric, body leaves the material plane but remains connected to the physical level of being. It is also possible, but much less usual, to pass to the higher spiritual realms when out of the body. In Near Death Experiences, it is usually the astral levels to which the ubiquitous "tunnel of light" leads. The soul may glimpse, but be turned back from, the spiritual levels beyond.

❧ The Chakras ❧

THE CHAKRAS ARE THE LINKAGE POINTS between the physical body and the subtle energy bodies. They can be seen quite clearly in the aura by those who have the ability to see beyond the physical. If the chakras are healthy, then the communication between the different energy bodies functions well. If they are not, then not only are the various levels not in harmony, but there is a danger of being open to "invasion" through the blocked chakras. For instance, if the solar plexus chakra is blocked or "stuck open," then you are at risk from energy leakage or psychic vampirism whereby someone else can leach out your energy. You will also soak up other people's emotional conditions. (We often instinctively try to protect this chakra by folding our arms across our midriff when we feel emotionally threatened or psychically drained.) If the third eye chakra is too open, you will be open to invasion from the astral levels, or from other people's thoughts. If there is an imbalance between the chakras: base chakra blocked, for instance, and crown chakra stuck open because of too much meditation without closing afterward, then you will feel ungrounded and spaced-out. By knowing how to close off, or protect, your chakras, you can avoid these problems.

In meditation, deliberately opening up the chakras increases the flow of spiritual energy. Protecting them afterwards ensures that the energy stays with us instead of flowing out to other people. When we interact intensely with other people, as in healing or counseling, we use our chakras to link and take in information. When we finish the interaction, we need not only to close off our chakras, but also to ensure that none of our energy has stayed with the other person, nor theirs with us.

Seen intuitively, the chakras appear like wheels, spinning around a vortex of light. Sometimes the chakras spin alternatively, one clockwise, the next counterclockwise. At other times they may all spin the same way. There is no one "right way." Seen psychically, the chakras should all have an equal rate of spin and give out the same amount of light and energy. One way to check this is to dowse with a pendulum. The rate of swing should be the same for each chakra. If the chakra is blocked, the visual effect may range from black energy spots within the chakra to a full shut-down where the chakra does not spin at all and looks very dark. Chakras which are wide open usually spin extremely fast, or they do not rotate but appear extremely bright with light spilling from them. If you are to maintain a healthy psychic equilibrium, it is vital to keep

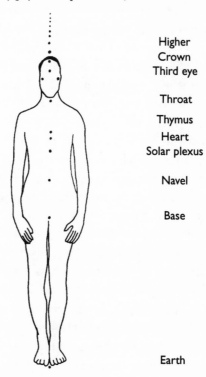

Higher
Crown
Third eye

Throat

Thymus
Heart
Solar plexus

Navel

Base

Earth

The Chakras.

your chakras cleansed, working properly and in balance with each other. The essence Bush Iris helps clear blocked chakras. Try taking it after checking your chakras with a pendulum. When you check again after taking the essence, there will be a noticeable difference.

In most systems, it is believed there are seven chakras ranged from the base of the spine up to the top of the head. However, there is a also a chakra below the feet, some additional chakras in the chest and head, and other chakras above the head which link to the spiritual levels. These additional chakras open as you evolve spiritually, and you will become aware of them as you progress and can incorporate them into your chakra visualizations when appropriate.

Being in touch with your earth chakra is an excellent way to keep yourself protected. It both grounds you and ensures that you are not too open on the spiritual level. Simply by reconnecting to this chakra at the end of meditation, you will automatically return fully into your physical body. As problems occur when people do not fully return, you will be preventing difficulty before it arises. You can also connect to this chakra before meditation. This allows you to bring the spiritual insights and energies down to the physical level, grounding them in practical, everyday life. It prevents you floating away and yet facilitates you opening fully to the spiritual energies at the same time, but without risk of psychic attack. If the kundalini force, a psychic and spiritual energy force that flows up the spine through the chakras and is stored at the base, starts to pulsate too strongly, direct it down to the earth chakra as otherwise it may "blow your mind" as it shoots up the spine.

The chakra opening and closing which follows can, once learned, be quickly carried out before and after meditation or other psychic work. Vibrationally, the Bush essence Red Lily cleanses the root chakra and opens the crown, enabling the spiritual energies to ground themselves into the body. A dose taken before the chakra exercises will be beneficial. The exercises should be followed by a dose of Fringed Violet and Flannel Flower to close down afterwards. The chakra protection should be practiced until it is automatic. Then you will be able to use it instantly when needed. It is sensible to use the cleansing visualization on a regular basis, and especially when you have been working with other people. The disentangling of chakras can be carried out when appropriate.

Chakras are usually pictured as lying along the spine but, for the exercises, you can picture them as being on the front or back of the body, whichever is easier. Traditionally, the chakras have been seen as many-petaled lotus flowers, but you can use any flower with which you feel comfortable.

These exercises should be carried out when you are relaxed and in a quiet, well-protected space. Ensure that you will not be disturbed while doing the exercise.

❧ Opening and Closing the Chakras

When you are ready to start your meditation, take your attention to the base of your spine and picture a tightly furled lotus bud unfolding and opening out petal by petal until it is a complete lotus, healthy and glowing with energy.

When that flower is fully open, move to the navel chakra. See the lotus bud sitting below your navel. Watch as it slowly opens.

When it is fully open, move your attention to the solar plexus. Picture the bud on a level with your midriff. See it slowly unfurling into its full beauty.

Then take your attention up to your heart. See the bud nestling in your heart. Watch as it opens into a full flower.

Move up to the throat. See the bud moving from tightly closed to fully opened flower.

Take your attention up to the third eye. The bud is between and slightly above your eyebrows. Watch as it opens petal by petal.

When it is fully open, take your attention to the top of the head, to the crown chakra. The bud here is large and full. Petal by petal it will open into a beautiful lotus flower ready to receive the spiritual energies at its center...

When you are ready to close after meditation, take your attention first to the crown chakra. Watch as the fully open lotus enfolds the spiritual energies at its heart and begins to close around them, returning to a tight bud-shaped form.

Then take your attention down to the third eye. Watch as this lotus slowly folds in on itself, closing back into a bud.

Then move down to the throat, seeing the flower close petal by petal until it is once more bud-like.

Then take your attention down to the heart. See the lotus flower in its center furling in on itself to form a bud once more.

Move down to the solar plexus. See this lotus closing in around its center until it once more assumes the bud-like, closed shape.

Then move to the navel chakra, seeing this lotus close itself up to protect its center.

Then move to the base chakra, allowing the lotus to gently fold in on itself to protect its energies.

If you are non-visual: Use your hands to simulate the opening and closing of each chakra in turn in front of the appropriate place on your body. Let yourself sense the chakra responding, opening and closing.

❦ Opening Chakras with Ground Chakra in Place

Begin by taking your attention down to your feet. Let your attention move on down into the ground a foot or so below your feet. You will find here an energy center that has a grounding cord that goes deep down into the earth. This cord holds you in incarnation. It is flexible, it allows you to move around, but it earths you and allows the energy of the earth to nourish and sustain you. Feel its energy, feel how it balances and stabilizes you.

This Earth chakra is linked to all the other chakras by an energy current. Keeping contact with the ground chakra, follow *this current up from the ground to the base of the spine. Maintain that contact with the Earth chakra as you move through the chakras up to the crown.*

Now go through the opening and closing of the chakras as in the preceding exercise...

Having closed and protected your chakras, take your attention down to your feet. Ensure that the Earth chakra is still open and functioning, its grounding cord still in place. Feel how it grounds you, brings you into your body. Feel how it allows you to go back into everyday life taking with you the spiritual insights you have gained through the meditation so that you can put them into practice.

Note: If you find yourself in a place which feels uncomfortable, maybe because of incompatible Earth energies, remember to protect your Earth chakra, enclosing it within a crystal to close it off and prevent it conveying any negative earth vibrations to you.

If you are non-visual: Stamp your foot to open and close the Earth chakra. Sense the current which links all the chakras flowing in through your feet and up through your body.

✦ Protecting the Chakras

Looking at each chakra in turn, picture it protected by twin doors which can open and close at your direction. Practice opening and closing each set of doors until it becomes an automatic process.

Let yourself sense which chakra is too open, which needs protection as you go about your daily life or into particular situations. Picture yourself in a situation, maybe meeting someone who drains your energy. Let yourself feel the difference protecting the appropriate chakra would make. Picture how it would be if the chakra were wide open. Then picture the result of closing the chakra doors. Remind yourself to close the doors when it is appropriate, so that it becomes automatic and you do not have to think about it.

Remember to check, in different situations, whether your chakra doors are open or closed.

If you are non-visual: Use your hands to simulate the doors opening and closing at the appropriate places.

❦ Cleansing the Chakras

With your eyes closed and your inner eye open, take your attention down to the base of the spine. Look at the base chakra. Is it spinning evenly with clear, bright light within it? Or is it murky, stuck, blocked? If there is a problem, use a whirlpool of light to cleanse, re-energize and rebalance the chakra. Let the whirlpool pull out any dark energy, see it get the chakra moving again, spinning around its light, bright center.

Then move the whirlpool up to the navel chakra and check this out. If it needs cleansing or unblocking, allow the whirlpool to do its work. Ensure that it is communicating with the base chakra, feel the energy flowing between the two.

Then move up in turn to the solar plexus, the heart, the throat, the third eye and the crown chakras. All should be spinning freely, full of light, and in communication with each other when the exercise is complete.

To finish the exercise, close the chakra doors until it is appropriate to open them again.

If you are non-visual: You can use a pendulum to check how the chakras are spinning. If they are uneven, place your hand over the spot and ask for the energy to be balanced. Then check again.

❦ Disentangling the Chakras

See the Tie Cutting on page 102.

The Higher Self

JUST AS WE HAVE AN "EVERYDAY SELF" that activates our body and lives life here on Earth (referred to throughout this book as our self), so too we have a "Higher Self" that inhabits the spiritual realm. This Higher Self is the eternal, immaterial part of our being: our divine essence, the seat of our higher consciousness, our spiritual being. It has many names: the self, the spirit, the god-within, the causal self, being just a few. (This can be confusing as the same terminology can cover different parts of our being according to the context and belief system to which it is applied.) Our Higher Self is more than our soul, our ego, our individuality. It is another vibratory dimension. It is "higher" because it is the part of our being that is vibrating fast enough to be in touch with the spiritual realm.

Through our Higher Self, we are linked to all that is. During a Near Death Experience, the classic tunnel experience takes us to a bright light and a being who awaits us. That being is very often our Higher Self, although we may not always recognize this, as the Higher Self may well appear as a "guide" or a religious figure with whom we can identify. It is the Higher Self who says, "Go back, it is not yet time for you to die" and who will frequently outline a task to be carried out, a lesson to be learned, an experience that is not yet completed.

The more we can contact, and embody, our Higher Self, the more we will raise our spiritual awareness, increase our vibratory level, and improve our protection in both the physical and the spiritual realms. This embodying of the Higher Self is important and is, I believe, the next evolutionary step for us humans. It means bringing our spiritual being into our physical being, into our life on Earth. For so many people, spiritual development means "transcending" the body—in other words, leaving it behind. But this can do great damage, and opens us to the possibility of possession by other entities or energies. While we are on Earth, we are meant to be living a physical life: we would not be here if we did not still have lessons to learn and tasks to do on this plane. When we have completed our lessons and our tasks, our soul and spirit are freed from the physical body to move onto another level of experience. Until this happens, we are not really free to leave the earth plane.

I well remember a friend of mine, who had been following the Ascension pathway, recounting an experience. He had been working on raising his vibrations (physical and spiritual) so that he could move into another dimension without having to die on this present one. He expected to take his physical body with him. However, in deep meditation, he left his body. He lost his connection with the physical level entirely. As he said: "I could have simply walked away. I knew I could not take this physical body into the new dimension but, inhabiting my spiritual body, I could have left the Earth plane for good. What stopped me was the sudden and yet absolute knowledge that, if I did leave, my physical body would continue to function. It was not yet time for that physical body to die. That physical body was part of me, so I was responsible for it. If I did not "caretake" that physical body, by living in it, I would not only be abusing that body but, as I was vividly aware, I would be leaving it to the mercy of other beings who would be only too happy to return to Earth and take it over. I simply could not do it. I knew I had to live as a totality, body and spirit." He chose to come back into his body and to work at raising its vibrations sufficiently to manifest his Higher Self in his everyday life.

It is possible to develop our contact with our Higher Self through meditation, chanting, ritual and pathworking, etc. But this must be grounded. We must literally embody the Higher Self by being in our body. We strengthen our ties with our physical body, purifying that body so that it can receive the raised vibrations of our spiritual self. We receive those vibrations only when we can encompass all the facets of our being: the "dark" as well as the "light," the unconscious as well as the superconscious. Like the yin and yang, we must have the balance. We do not embody our Higher Self by running away from the physical side of life into the spiritual. This results in someone who has, at most, a toehold on earth—a very tenuous link through which the spiritual can manifest. Nor do we embody it by becoming a saccharin sweet "goody-goody" who talks of light and love, and totally represses half of their being. A half which will, inevitably, surface later with great force, tearing them, and anyone around them, asunder in the process. Only when stable and integrated on the physical, emotional/psychological, mental, and spiritual levels of our being can we truly bring our higher spiritual energies into play. However, the more we reach up to our Higher Self, the more we can hear that voice within, and the greater strength we will have.

❧ Reaching up to the Higher Self

Sit quietly for a few moments, consciously sending out the thought that your Higher Self will be with you. Imagine a beam of bright, white light going out from the crown chakra at the top of your head, through the chakras above your head, and reaching up to your Higher Self. Allow the energies of your Higher Self to reach you through this column of light. These energies are all-loving and all-encompassing. There is great compassion and empathy in the Higher Self. It accepts and loves us as we are. You may well hear an inner voice speaking to you, or simply be aware of a non-verbal communication. Allow yourself as much time as you need.

When you are ready to return, consciously close down the chakras as the light beam retracts. Then check that your grounding cord is in place and that you are once more attuned to the energies of the earth.

Once you have established this contact with your Higher Self, simply sending out that beam of light will put you in touch whenever you need it.

❧ Meeting the Higher Self

(This exercise should be taped and played for as many sessions as it takes you to be able to step out at the top of the elevator in full consciousness of what is happening. If you need it, include the instructions for relaxation on page 134.)

Settle yourself comfortably and relax...

When you are ready, picture yourself entering a high-speed elevator that goes way up out of sight into the clouds. Press the button marked "top" and allow the elevator to take you up as high as it can go.

When the elevator stops, step out. You will find that your Higher Self has come to meet you. Embrace your Higher Self. Feel the loving energies enclosing you. Spend as much time as necessary with your Higher Self...

When it is time to return, ask your Higher Self to enter the elevator with you. (This may or may not be possible at this time.) Press the button marked "Ground" and allow the elevator to return you to everyday consciousness. Step out of the elevator and into the everyday world once more. (With practice and perseverance, you will be able to see your Higher Self stepping out of the elevator with you.)

Move your hands and feet. Take a few deeper breaths. Open your eyes. Get up and walk around the room, deliberately placing your feet on the earth and allowing yourself to feel the connection to the Earth as strongly as possible.

It is quite usual when working with this exercise to find you have "lost consciousness" of what has happened somewhere between entering the elevator and reaching the top. You think you went to sleep, got nowhere, etc. Persevering and asking to remember will help you to bring the memory back. You can put an instruction onto the tape as you enter the elevator to remind you to ask your Higher Self for an object or symbol that you bring back with you. When you step out of the elevator again, include the instruction to look and see what your Higher Self has given you. You will be surprised to see that you have brought something back. As you learn to retain awareness in those higher realms, you will bring back more and more memory of what goes on there.

If you are working on embodying the Higher Self, when you embrace the Higher Self, become one. Practice coming back in the elevator as one being. Eventually you will be able to step out of the elevator at ground level fully embodying your Higher Self and bringing this into your everyday life.

≀ The Power of Thought ≀

THOUGHT IS THE MOST POWERFUL FORCE on this planet. Thought is the impulse that sets things in motion, that creates, that annihilates. We have beauty because someone had a thought. We have the possibility of nuclear war because someone else had a different one. The one contains the seed of the other. If only we could fully understand the power of thought, we could recreate our world. If we truly knew that "as a man thinks, so he is," we could become the most perfectly evolved beings ever known.

Thought is therefore a potent tool in our psychic armory. What we believe in, we bring into being. To believe in ourselves is our strongest protection. If we know, at the deepest level of our being, that nothing can touch us, then we have perfect protection. If we realize that thoughts are things, then we will cease to inflict harm both on ourselves and others. If we can recognize a thought form, then a stronger thought by us can wink it out of existence. If we find ourselves out of our body, we can think ourselves back in.

Some people are, of course, more sensitive to thought than others. But we have all at one time or another had the experience of having a thought pop into our head that wasn't ours. We have picked it up telepathically from the psychic airwaves. Some people are constantly bombarded, for others it is a rare event. But it happens. How often depends on how open our aura is. It is this permeability of our "mindfield" that makes us vulnerable to psychic attack—that, and our own belief system.

The power of the curse is ancient and omniscient. No one can hear themselves cursed in even the most mild of forms

without a visceral stirring of fear. When I lived ir
in the bush, I had a house boy who was cursed by u...
(the local witchdoctor). This *ju-ju* was clearly powerful. W..
they built the airport, the (European) contractors were surprised to learn that they could not site a hanger on the path
where the *ju-ju* walked. They did. It fell down overnight. They
built it again. It fell down again. They moved it. It stayed up.
So, when my house boy was cursed for some minor misde-
meanor, he became ill overnight. His belief system could have
it no other way. Our English doctor could find nothing wrong
and said it was fear-induced. The doctor had been in the trop-
ics a long time and respected the power of belief and that of the
ju-ju, which he had seen heal as well as curse. My house boy
had been educated at the Catholic mission school. So, the doctor gave him a religious amulet and told him it had the power
to dissolve the curse. The "white man's medicine" was more
powerful. As the boy had been indoctrinated into believing
that the white man's religion was the ultimate power, and that
the white man reigned supreme (these were colonial days), it
overcame his tribal belief in the *ju-ju*. But that belief had, for a
time, triumphed despite his education.

It is this fear, this primitive-brain response, that makes the
curse work. Part of us takes it in, believes it, and manifests the
consequences. This is why chain letters have such insidious
power. We receive the first one with its dire threats of death
and disaster if we don't pass it on. We crumple it up, put it on
the fire, or throw it in the trash. "It can't hurt us" is our belief
at this stage: although even here we may hesitate just for a
moment... "Can it?" Then, a few days later we have a minor
disaster. Suddenly we remember that letter and we begin to
wonder. Did it have power? Has it caused this? We give it
power simply by allowing that doubt to creep in. Our belief system subtly alters. It might, perhaps, have the power to hurt us.
No, our rational mind intervenes, of course it does not. But,

below the level of the rational mind, in the older, primeval part of our being, that possibility is stored. It gets activated when the next letter arrives, and the next, no matter how long the interval. The causal chain becomes strong as incidents that we could, in other circumstances, overlook, become attached to the letters. Even though our rational mind does not believe, that more primitive part of us is overriding it. Now we hesitate before we crumple it up, we waver. We are hooked.

Where the curse, or the attack, is purely at the psychic or telepathic level, it bypasses our rational belief system altogether and goes straight to the primitive, irrational level. So, we don't actually need to know we are cursed for the attack to trigger fear and psychic consequences. Nor do we need an outside source: our own fear can induce the same consequences because our primitive brain believes in them, and what we believe we manifest.

Such irrational beliefs cannot simply be ignored. We cannot will ourselves into believing differently. After all, this is a psychic inheritance from our remotest ancestors. It is deeply programmed into our subconscious mind. But we can subtly reprogram those beliefs and satisfy them through ritual, the process by which our ancestors kept their primitive fears and so-called irrational superstitions at bay. Use of a ritual over a long time imbues it with power to overcome fear. Catholics cross themselves to ward off evil, an ancient ritual. Egyptians still wear the Eye of Horus for protection, part of an even more ancient ritual.

It is the process of allowing fear and doubt in, that makes us vulnerable to our own negative belief in ourselves and to other people's beliefs about us—and to other's greater or lesser malevolent intent. Parents program their children: "This one is different from all the rest. He's so naughty/clumsy/aggressive/thick/etc." Then they are surprised when "he" turns out to be an anti-social loner who mugs old ladies for his drug money! We do this to ourselves all the time. We have some very deep, irrational beliefs about ourselves that reside out of our usual consciousness. But, from the depths of our psyche, they subtly undermine what we try to do. "I don't deserve to be...," "I'm not worthy to be...," "I will never be..." ensure that we never will be. On the other hand, "Why does it always happen to me," ensures that it always will. As Richard Bach says, "Argue your limitations and sure enough they are yours." We manifest what we believe.

The single thought "He or she is more powerful than me" lays us open to psychic dominance. Such an attack may not be malevolently meant. "Poor old so-and-so...," said out of sympathy and repeated often enough, will ensure poverty and ill fortune for the rest of so-and-so's natural life—if so-and-so believes that he or she is powerless, helpless and at the mercy of outside forces. If, deep down, so-and-so believes he or she is all-powerful and in control of life, then the situation could change dramatically overnight.

So, by learning to focus our thoughts and to program them to be positive rather than negative, we create our protection. (This can be enhanced by the use of a turquoise crystal as it not only protects but promotes positive thought.) This is the power behind creative visualization. It is not the images that work, it is the concentrated thought we put into creating them that brings the results. The pictures are merely a focus for our intention. This is why "acting as if" is so important when you have difficulty in visualizing. If you let yourself feel the process, listen to the inner voice, act as though you are seeing, have the intention, then thought acts on your belief.

The reverse process is used by those who attack. They focus, consciously or unconsciously, their resentment, rage and hatred into a concentrated ball of thought which hurtles towards their victim through the psychic air waves. If that "victim" has no protection, it slams into their mindfield with tremendous force. If the "victim" has strong protection, it can bounce off onto those around (one of the reasons why your children's protection should be boosted regularly, especially if you have reason to believe you may come under psychic attack). So, if you know you are under attack, defensive techniques which create a restraining thought barrier as close to the perpetrator as possible should be used. It will then bounce back to its source.

When boosting your psychic protection, or using any technique, your first thought should be "I can do this. I have the power." If you notice yourself wobbling in your belief about this, go over to a mirror. Stand as close to the mirror as possible and look yourself straight in the eye. Look into the depths of your eyes, go as deep as possible: the eyes are the window of the soul and a doorway to your higher powers. Say firmly, out loud, "I can do this. I do have the power." Keep looking in those eyes, and repeat it until you believe it with all your heart and soul. Your mind will follow. Any stray thoughts such as "Oh yes, who says," "But...," can be blasted out of existence with a psychic laser gun. Use your power, that is what it is there for! How do you find a psychic laser gun? You think it into existence, that's how. You picture it, imagine it, visualize it, until you can feel it in your hand. Then you apply it to the doubting thought and, poof, it disappears. If you believe in yourself, you can do it.

However, don't become too blasé or egotistical. Pride always goes before a fall in psychic work. And, as like attracts like, you will set yourself up as a target for a psychic power struggle sooner or later. Much better to retain your humility. Your belief in yourself and your ability to protect yourself should give you a quiet confidence, not a bombastic arrogance that says: "I know it all, I can do it all." We need to remain flexible. If we become too rigid or arrogant, the thoughts we are putting out will attract to us people who are themselves rigid and arrogant. They, too, know best. If we are smug and overconfident, we will attract someone who says, "Ah, but I can do it better." As thoughts are tangible things on the psychic airwaves, battle will commence.

ꙅ Like Attracts Like ꙅ

WE KNOW FROM PARTICLE PHYSICISTS, and the ancient mystics, that the universe is in constant motion. Just as the planets of our solar system revolve around the sun, so does matter form itself out of the raw materials of existence. Some of this matter is dense, other diffuse, depending on the degree of attraction holding it together. Other particles of matter are rushing away from one another at great speed; they have been repulsed. As everything is vibration, there is an attraction-repulsion force at work throughout all the different levels of being.

Psychically, this means that whatever energies we are putting out, we will attract back to us. Whatever our frequency is, our rate of vibration, we will attract beings at a similar rate, and repulse those who are not. Whatever thoughts we are putting out will create our reality, good or bad. If we expect peace and harmony at the deepest level of our being, this is what we will get. If that belief is superficial and, underneath, even the smallest part of us does not trust the universe, then we will experience disharmony and disturbance. If we put out fear, we will attract fearsome things back.

This principle holds good at all levels of psychic work. If we have raised our vibrations to the highest possible level, lower vibrations cannot stick: we may experience them but will not be caught by them. If our intention is to the highest good (and not contaminated by egotistical thoughts of self-glory), then we will achieve that good. If our thoughts are pure (not saccharin sweet or sanctimonious) then we will manifest good.

The principle of "like attracts like" really helps in meditation and psychic work, in that, if we keep our thoughts and our vibrations at the highest level, then we can travel safely. Nothing can touch us. We will be protected no matter what realms we may traverse. If we can raise our vibrations to their highest level, then we can reach out to our Higher Self, that part of us that is at its highest vibration.

Vibration can also be used as a tool. Sound is a vibration. So, we can use music to help us raise the vibrations. There are excellent meditation pieces available. If you find one that really fits, you can make a point of playing it. It then becomes a ritual, and rituals are profoundly protective. Music induces trance states. Used repetitively, it will take you to higher states of consciousness. You can also use music to alter mood or atmosphere. If you sense that someone is thinking about you with not altogether pleasant thoughts, you can block it out with music. If you feel troubled, uneasy, unaccountably angry, you can soothe yourself with the right piece of music. This changes the vibrations you are putting out, and alters what you are attracting back to yourself.

We need a balance however. Too much attraction, a surfeit of sweetness and light, smothers and stagnates us. If we always repress our dark side, then what we attract back will be other people's blackness. But, at its core, it is really our own.

⁊ Thought Forms ⁊

SOME YEARS AGO A TEAM OF AMERICAN parapsychology researchers performed a somewhat bizarre, but highly successful experiment. They thought a communicator "from the other side" into existence. They visualized him and his life history into being. He was, in fact, a totally fictitious character but they created a life for him. The communicator then presented, through a series of mediums, the exact details of his life as scripted by the researchers. It was a life he had never actually lived, because he was, technically, a figment of their collective imagination. But he lived in thought. He was a thought form.

Writers are all too familiar with this process. The characters from novels or scripts are noted for taking on a life of their own. They behave in a certain way not because the author wants them to, but because they have to. That is the way they are. With millions of stories having been told, somewhere out there on the psychic airwaves are all the characters. If the story is filmed, the actor has to fit the reader's expectations. He has to take on the character because it already exists, in thought. If he doesn't, the film fails.

In the Tibetan Bardo (an afterlife state), exist the "hungry ghosts." These are formed from all the unsatisfied desires of humankind. Desires are powerful thoughts. They create, they have life. The hungry ghosts too are thought forms. On Earth, ghosts are thought forms. They are like a psychic photograph left behind. Usually created out of deep misery or extreme anger, they imprint themselves on a place, are caught in the moment, and remain to haunt the living. They rarely communicate and have little psychic energy, unless someone comes along who believes in them strongly, or who fears them. This "feeds" them and they become stronger. They are very different to lost souls who have not yet found their way properly over to the other side of death. They are caught in limbo land but exist in their own right, not as thought forms.

Magicians throughout the ages have deliberately created thought forms to work for them; such forms do not have to be humanlike. Witches' "familiars" were thought forms that, usually, assumed animal shape but could change and travel as necessary, directed by the mind of the witch. If a magician wanted to attack, he would create "demons and devils" to do the work for him. He would call on incubus and succubus for aid in his magical working. Many spells, too, relied on thought forms. Thought took shape, and did its work.

But, you don't need to be a trained magician to create a thought form (but perhaps you were, in a former life). Whenever we desire something strongly enough, we create it on the mental level. Whenever we send out an envious or destructive thought, it exists on that level. We are linked by thought. This is why so much psychic attack is unconscious. Unless people know the power of thought, they do not know that they are creating something that will have a life of its own. Something that will home in on its target. Thought forms are fueled by strong emotion: jealousy, anger, envy, hatred. But they can equally well be fueled by love, and a desire to protect ourselves. So, whenever you become aware of putting out a strong thought to someone else, especially if this is to harm them, always ask that the thought be neutralized. Karmically, it is not wise to put out harmful thoughts, as they will always return to their source one way or another. The more spiritually aware we become, the quicker the karma comes round. So, for your own protection, avoid such thoughts.

When I came under psychic attack, it was powerful because it was fueled by some very dark emotions indeed, and it was made by two people who had trained their minds to heal. A trained mind has more power to focus, and can just as easily be used for ill as for good. They, inadvertently or deliberately, created thought forms that continued the attack whether the perpetrators were actively engaged in it or not. My partner, in creating the Sekhmet Guardians (see page 44), also created thought forms which would go on working without our attention. It was the withdrawing of my attention, the disengaging of my energies, that enabled me to extricate myself. The thought forms continued to protect me—they still do, but not in such a fearsome aspect.

We need to be aware of thought forms not only because we may inadvertently create or attract them, but also because we may meet them in our astral travels. Being forewarned is being forearmed. Sometimes what we meet is the product of our own fears or an over active imagination—too many horror stories can create fearsome monsters. They may be in our imagination, but we still have to deal with them. But, out there, on the psychic level, we meet the products of other people's nightmares too.

To meet thought forms was one of the stages initiates had to go through—knowing that, although the forms appeared to have life, they were not real. I vividly remember reliving an initiation in Egypt. Having been prepared, I was placed "in a tomb" and sealed in. I was motionless, in deep trance, possibly drugged, maybe just hypnotized or in telepathic contact with the minds of the priests. It wasn't clear. What was clear was that, left alone, I was out of my body. I had a series of classic tests to overcome: a pit of snakes, a multitude of forms to subdue by the power of mind and spirit. I had to know I was safe, indestructible. If I believed these forms were real, I was lost. If I disbelieved in them and believed in my own protection, I was safe. I also had guardians to call on. (Perhaps this is why I use Sekhmet now.)

Since then, I have read innumerable accounts of similar experiences. I have taken people back through initiations. I have "seen" for clients the effects of a failed initiation, what happens when the thought forms prevail, and we have been back into that life together to overcome it. I believe that some schizophrenics are tuning into this memory, individual or collective, and the thought forms associated with it. Other people meet them in meditation or astral travel. Some of those priestly thought forms still exist—anyone who doubts this should spend some time alone in the subterranean crypts at Dendera. However, they can be winked out of existence (with psychic lasers and disbelief) or ignored. The danger comes in believing in them.

When I was asked by Findhorn Press what kind of cover illustration I would like for this book, I immediately thought of a painting of Sekhmet I have in my study. I knew that its creator, Judith Page, has strong links with Sekhmet herself. When I expressed my interest, Judith felt that Sekhmet was perhaps the wrong choice for the cover as she knew Sekhmet in the guise of a healer. She suggested Sobek, the guardian and protector crocodile god. She had a painting which had been created specifically for its protective energies. When she sent me a copy, to my surprise it was the same illustration that I had cut out of a magazine a few days earlier. I had met Sobek when under psychic attack (see page 44); as he was being used against me, he was not my first thought for a guardian being. However, as I completed this book, it became apparent to me that I needed to make friends with him to help heal the past. I had placed the magazine cutting on my collage of "things I want to achieve in the coming year." He symbolized reconciliation and regeneration of my psychic energies. Now, in the period between Christmas and New Year, here was Judith offering Sobek painted at his moment of rebirth and renewal. He was to be the protector of the book I had just birthed. It seemed perfect synchronicity and exactly the right choice.

Having a guardian being with you protects against thought forms, so it is well worth creating a guardian long before the need arises. That way, you can call on your guardian whenever there is a need.

Sekhmet.

⸙ To Create Your Guardian

*Choose a guardian being in whom you believe and with whom
you have a resonance. You may like to select an archangel, an
angelic being, a mythological character, a god or goddess, an animal, or a person. Whatever feels right for you.*

*Then, find some pictures of your intended guardian or maybe
a statue. (Illustrator Judith Page has some wonderful paintings of
appropriate beings, see useful addresses page 144) Draw it for
yourself. (It doesn't have to be a masterpiece; it is the intention
behind the drawing that is important.) Keep these pictures with
you. Refer to them from time to time until they become familiar.
You may find a piece of music, special colors, crystals (a celestine
under the pillow attracts our guardian angel), objects or flowers
that relate to your guardian. Use anything that will help to bring
this being closer to you.*

Then, when you are ready, settle yourself quietly with your pictures, crystals, etc. Take time to relax, to focus your attention deep inside yourself, to let the outside world slip away, to move into your inner world.

Look at the picture, focus all your attention on it. See the living being behind the static image. When the picture is imprinted on your mind, close your eyes and continue to hold the image, seeing it clearly with your inner eye. Feel the life force in that image, imbue it with energy, see it come alive. Focus all your attention on that living being.

Welcome your guardian. Ask for protection and strength. Ask that your guardian will be there whenever you need help or refuge. Clearly state your purpose in bringing your guardian into being and ensure that your guardian consents.

Spend time together getting comfortable. You may like to arrange some kind of signal or symbol that will enable you to call on your guardian instantly in time of need. You may ask the guardian for a name. Whatever you feel you need.

When you have spent enough time with your guardian, thank it for coming, and ask it to be there when needed.

Switch your attention back into the room, leaving your guardian in your inner eye. Check that your cloak of protection is in place and that you are fully occupying your body. Get up and walk around the room, reconnecting to the earth.

Practice calling your guardian a few times before there is a need, that way you will know that you are protected.

If you are non-visual: Ask your guardian to communicate by feel or touch. Sense the presence rather than see it. Ask for a signal rather than a symbol: my head used to prickle and I'd feel a touch on my shoulder long before I saw anything. I would feel a cloak dropped around me to protect me before I consciously recognized that I needed it.

ᛉ Invoking Sobek* as Protector

Settle yourself comfortably, holding the book in your hands. When you are ready, let yourself focus on the cover illustration. Sobek is painted at his moment of rebirth and renewal. Energy crackles all around him. In his hands, he holds the ancient flint knives, instruments of ritual protection, which belonged to the first man. With these knives, Sobek is invincible. He will smite your enemies for you, either with knives or with bolts of lightning.

As you focus on Sobek, feel him come to life. Be with him as he moves. Switch to your inner eye. See the world through his eyes. Experience his invulnerability, his strength, his calm knowing and certainty, his power.

When he turns to look at you, be ready. Humbly ask him to be your guardian, your protector. Petition, do not demand. Remember to ask him what he needs from you. He is a god of Ancient Egypt, used to offerings of respect and replenishment. If you honor him, he will fulfill your needs. Treat him without honor, misuse him, and you may feel his terrible energy directed towards you instead. But, if you come as supplicant, prepared to make the offerings a god demands, he will be your loyal and invincible protector.

Spend time attuning to Sobek, becoming comfortable with him...

When you have completed your meeting, bring your awareness back into the room and open your eyes. Check that your cloak of protection is around you and resume your normal activities.

If you are non-visual: Keep Sobek's picture on hand to call on him.

---

* Sobek is used on the cover of this book.

❧ Dissolving Thought Forms

Laughter and disbelief are potent forces in disempowering thought forms. Laughing at something dissolves it. If you truly don't believe in it, it will not be there. But we cannot always summon up that degree of disbelief. Our fear gets in the way. When we can overcome our fear, we are protected. In the meantime, we can equip ourselves with a useful defensive tool.

I have learned many techniques for dissolving thought forms over the years, but my favorite came spontaneously when watching *Star Trek* many moons ago. Its advantage is that it is quick and very easy to use. A psychic laser, or phaser, has a beam of energy that dissolves matter instantly if required. That its fuel is concentrated thought energy does not really concern us. That its guidance system is our will, does. It is the power of your intention that will make it work.

Once you have created the phaser, it will always be there for use. It has different settings so you need not totally annihilate with it. "Stun" is often sufficient, or you may want to use its powers to transport something to another galaxy, or just out of your way. You don't have to be able to "see" the phaser to use it, just to know it is there. Thought forms are not always visible; you are more likely to feel their presence, so taking instinctive aim solves the problem of "not seeing." Let your will, your intent, propel it to where its force is needed.

❧ The Psychic Phaser

Picture a small black object in your hand. Feel its weight, its roundness, smoothness. Look at it, feel it. You will see several settings, which simply need a thought to change them.

In the center is a big red button. Press it, and a beam of energy shoots out to your target, dissolving, disabling or transporting as required. (When you get really good at this, you won't even have to use your finger to press the button, thought will do it for you.)

Then "think up" a belt on which to hang this phaser. Put it on and always wear it, no matter where you are. Then it will be to hand—practice thinking it into your hand and back onto the belt until it becomes automatic. Have target practice until even an unseen object is hit, instantly and accurately every time.

Remember it in your time of need.

You may also like to extend this to another useful *Star Trek* piece of equipment—the deflector shield. *The Enterprise* is protected by a powerful shield that neutralizes anything that is thrown at it. So, you too can be surrounded by a deflector shield. The outer edge of your aura can be automatically programmed to neutralize harmful forces from any source. Action follows thought. Imagine the shield, and it will exist.

⁊ Psychic Attack ⁊

PSYCHIC ATTACK IS SOMETHING THAT I tend not to believe in, until I am forcibly reminded. I find I easily forget just how over-powering it can be. Fortunately I have, as far as I know, only come under such attack three times. But I have been on the receiving end of the odd resentful and vengeful thought from time to time, just often enough to remind me to keep my protection up. I have also worked with many people who have come under varying degrees of psychic attack.

During my training with Christine Hartley, I learned to drive a car. Christine immediately said: "You must put a pentagram around yourself for protection." Being a literal Sagittarian I did exactly that, drew a mental five-pointed star over my head every time I climbed into the car. Several months later I had a spectacular car accident in the snow, landing upside down several feet above the road. I was unhurt. The car was a write-off. I asked Christine what had gone wrong. "Did you protect the car?," she asked. "No," said I. "Well, do it next time," she said.

A year or so later I inadvertently upset a rather powerful man—Sagittarians are born with their foot in their mouth and I said the wrong thing. At the time I was not aware that he was a practicing magician—but I did notice a distinct cooling of the atmosphere round me, and a tendency to minor domestic accidents. I stepped up my protection, just in case, but thought no more about it. A week later I was in the outside lane of a highway, with my daughter and two old ladies aboard. A car came on from a side road, swung right over to the outside lane and hit us broadside on. Apart from wavering a little, my car kept on going. "That's broken a dream," said my daughter, "I dreamed we were in your old car and another car hit us and we landed upside down in the opposite lane."

I might not have associated this with psychic attack except that coincidentally (not that I believe in coincidence, I prefer to call it synchronicity), a friend called to say he had had exactly the same accident at around the same time. He mentioned he had also upset the same man as I had, but rather more seriously. Being aware of this, he had maintained protection around himself. In his case, it was an eighteen-wheeler that side-swiped him, but he was unhurt and his car, as with mine, escaped with a dented door. We were not sure whether it was malicious attack or out-of-control raging thoughts that had created the accidents, but we were sure we knew who was at the bottom of it.

Now, whenever and however I travel, I surround myself and the passengers with individual pentagrams, and the transport itself with a huge one. I have had some very near misses, but no more accidents, and I travel thousands of miles each year.

Almost twenty years went by before I triggered the enormous rage of a well-known "New Age" figure. I was told I would lance the poison in his soul, and I certainly did. During his ranting and raving, he threatened to destroy me. He was backed up by a powerful woman cohort. I was overwhelmed by a malevolent wave of ill will flowing toward me. This time I knew it was a deliberate attack and threw everything I had into protecting myself. He, and his cohort, were very effective healers and what heals can be turned to destructive purposes. Not that I really believed he had the power to do this. However, I seriously underestimated their combined abilities. By the end of six months I was on my knees, totally drained, I could not work and everything in my life was going wrong. I decided to go to Egypt to get away from it all. I simply could not be bothered to fight them any longer.

Almost the first thing I saw in Egypt was a huge, newly exca-
vated statue of a crocodile (minus its head): Sobek, who was in
my then recent experience an agent of ancient evil, but who
was later revealed in his role of protector. "There you are," said
my partner matter-of-factly, "That's her dealt with, and he is
powerless without her." I laughed till my sides hurt, and laughter is wonderful cleanser. The reason I laughed so much was
that, having exhausted my repertoire, my partner had sent several 120-foot high statues of the lion-headed goddess Sekhmet,
menstruating and dripping blood from her fangs (Scorpios
have such vivid imaginations), to patrol my attackers' home
territory. Sekhmet was sent as a guardian, protective being; she
was instructed not to attack unless provoked. We had joked
about a clash of the gods from ancient Egypt because, somehow the cohort had always appeared to us psychically in the
guise of Sobek and the guru as Set, his master. From the
moment I saw that statue, I felt better. My health, and my life,
started to improve. I came home from Egypt a different person.

When I began to look at it objectively, I realized that I had
been expending enormous energy "defending myself" rather
than just keeping my protection up. I had let it in too close to
me, become too involved. I was sucked in and did not maintain my distance and detachment. I gave it considerable
attention; in fact, it was rarely out of my mind. Now I wonder
how much of it I created by that attention. I was also aware
that the protection was too specific to the man involved. I did
not, at first, know that there was also a woman helping him
and her energies were able to get in close to me because all my
energy was directed at keeping him out. I also realized that I
was particularly vulnerable because, having been threatened,
I subconsciously allowed fear in. I knew this was an extremely
angry and violent person, although for much of the time this
anger was repressed under a thin veneer of "love." He could
well have physically confronted me, and so I was worried.
Being worried and frightened not only opens up channels

through which the other person's psychic energy can reach us, but can cause us to create exactly what we fear most. Indeed, many curses and so-called spells rely on the power of autosuggestion. They do not work if the person concerned is not aware of them. Most of the effect comes from the victim's own imagination and power of thought.

In this case, I was using a technique that included sending love to them, trying to change the energy, something I had used with great effect on other occasions. But, I soon realized, they were picking up this love and turning it around into psychic energy to fuel the battle. It was only when I gave up, and withdrew my energy, that I was freed.

While I was writing this book, my partner reminded me that, having become involved by sending the Sekhmets, one day he experienced a total energy drain, "Like someone had pulled out the plug." I was out at the time, when I arrived home I realized that the terrible twosome were lecturing locally and had been sending particularly strong thoughts to the house. He sent a temporary Sekhmet to the lecture hall, and asked her to accompany them home. His energy was immediately restored. I include this because, whatever method of defense you choose, it should not be tied to a specific place— the mistake my partner made. It should be linked to the person who is putting out the bad vibes.

These are extreme examples, and yet they are the experience of many, many people. As soon as I started work on this book, as though to confirm the need for it, an astrology workshop participant told an horrendous story of a twelve-year psychic attack. From which, although she was well-protected, she had still not quite disentangled herself. She needed a tie cutting with the person concerned. Other people have similar stories. A doctor running a drug-abuse clinic treated a young girl who had gotten entangled with some rather strange people. The doctor found herself literally helpless, unable to drag herself to the phone. The group was directing negative energy at her. They wanted their member back. Fortunately someone stopped by her apartment, realized there was a problem and sought help. She was given a black tourmaline to wear, which as well as deflecting negative energy attack also helps to ground the person wearing it. Her energy came back and she had no more problems.

A healer working with a well-known healing group aroused the envy of another member of the group. Eventually she came to me and said, "Can you take the knife out of my back?" The other person's thoughts had become so strong, so focused, it felt exactly like a knife between the shoulder blades. As the healer said, she had learned that being psychic or a healer does not necessarily make someone a spiritually oriented person. Unfortunately, there is as much backbiting and animosity within spiritual groups as in any other. So simply belonging to a spiritual group is not protection in itself. Other psychic attack experiences are less dramatic, but just as debilitating. Sometimes the source of the attack is known, often it is not. If you are terrified of the thought of coming under psychic attack, the Bush essence Grey Spider Flower will help you to develop trust that you will be protected. A smoky quartz crystal helps to calm fear, so wear one or keep one in your pocket.

If you are on the receiving end of ill will or bad thoughts, you can mentally place a mirror close to the person to reflect it back—he or she usually begins to feel very ill indeed, often within hours. As someone once commented, "It gives a whole new meaning to getting your own back." If you are aware of thought energy invading your home, then an actual mirror can be positioned to direct it back to its source. With the "New Age" guru mentioned above, I had to move the mental mirror closer and closer until eventually I used a large tin, mirrored on the inside, into which I popped him and then chained the lid. I have particularly graphic visual imagery and "saw" this tin bulging and straining (rather like Popeye's spinach can about to burst). It needed a ton of chains to keep it in place as his anger fed on itself. When I eventually cut my link with it, he went down like a spent balloon. Having little real power of his own, he fed on other people's. Removing the energy left him powerless.

To absorb negative thoughts, you can picture a ball of cottonwool-like substance between you and the other person. You can then picture burning it to transmute the negative energies, or washing them away with water. A variation on this, which works well with negative emotions, is the "purple bubble," "red bubble," etc., according to what the emotion is that is coming your way (red for anger, purple for resentment, green for jealousy, and so on). The bubble, which does not touch you, magnetically attracts the emotion to it. When it can hold no more, it floats away high into the sky like a balloon and is pricked to release what it carries as harmless droplets spreading over a wide area. My partner, who is scientifically trained, likes to imagine a wide barrier of lead either side of a vacuum between himself and the other person. He feels that this will blot out any emanations.

Crystals also work well to deflect negative thoughts. You can keep one near you at all times or wear it. A black obsidian will absorb negative energies. Jet is an excellent shield, as is black jade. Or you can wear an amethyst or quartz crystal around your neck. These stones have traditionally been worn for this purpose for thousands of years.

If the attack is not too severe, simply surrounding the person with loving thoughts can work dramatically well. It can bring about a complete turnaround. The key is to maintain the love steadily, giving it attention from time to time and focusing on seeing that person well, happy, and full of loving thoughts. This does not work unless it really comes from your heart. You must be lovingly dispassionate. If you have any doubts or deeply hidden feelings of animosity, it will fail. Nor can you will it into being. That means controlling the other person and this is against spiritual law.

In an ideal world, we would have loving relationships and no angry thoughts, so inadvertent psychic attack would be rare. We are, unfortunately, a long way from this, but one of the best ways to prevent psychic attack is to teach people from an early age just how powerful thoughts are. In the meantime, keeping your own protection up with a strong aura is a good way to ensure that nothing gets through. The Green Pyramid exercise (see page 52) works well against psychic attack, as does The Mummy, but you can also find your own protective images or symbols. A symbol should be something deeply meaningful for you, something you can instantly call on. A cross or crucifix works well for people with a Christian orientation. I find the goddess Sekhmet very handy, myself.

The subtle vibrational healing of flower essences can be extremely helpful in cases of psychic attack (see page 119). A combination of the Bush essences Grey Spider Flower and Fringed Violet not only protects against the fear and terror of the attack, but also strengthens and repairs the aura, our natural defense.

Not all psychic attack comes from outside ourselves. If we have been consistently ignoring or rejecting parts of our self, it may be mirrored back to us through the actions of another person, but it will be *our* psychic disturbance. It may be experienced as overwhelming fear or phobias arising seemingly out of nowhere, but it is coming from inside us. Exploring these neglected facets of ourselves may be necessary. Instead of "defending against" these factors, we may need to welcome them into our consciousness. This process needs a skilled guide or therapist, but a malachite crystal helps to draw out our own negativity and a milky quartz puts us in touch with our own subconscious mind, while a black obsidian draws our buried fears to the surface. I have always found psychosynthesis works well, but other approaches are equally valid. "Know thyself" was one of the great precepts of the Delphic Oracle. It is as valid today as it was then. To know our self fully is one of the best forms of protection available, as it minimizes our vulnerability to psychic attack, both inner and outer. Here again, flower essences can help as they gently release the blocked emotions and disturbed psychic states that lie deep in our subconscious mind. A qualified practitioner should be consulted but some useful first aid remedies are included in the section on the essences.

Nor is psychic attack necessarily from people currently alive. I was once asked for help by a group of teenage punks. They had been playing with a Ouija board in a disused police station, and had stirred up some most unpleasant energies—and entities. These included the soul of a murderer who had died of a heart attack in the station (a fact later confirmed by research). He was angry, and delighted to have found a way to express it. Poltergeist activity was a particular problem because one of the youths lived in the building and was bombarded by all kinds of flying objects. It was in his room that the Ouija board had been used, and this room remained the focus of activity, although all the group experienced objects moving around them at one time or another. They all suffered from nightmares, were aware of invasive, destructive thoughts that were not theirs, and became increasingly depressed.

When I went in, there were two priorities. One was to move this soul, and several others, on. The other was to give the group instant protection. Then we could move onto clearing the space and cleaning up the energies of the building.

We worked on strengthening the aura and on creating a safe space in which to work by using The Light technique, burning incense and placing crystals around. The latter were mainly props to reassure the punks and create the right ambiance, but I do find crystals absorb negative energies and help with the clearing. I then asked the group to sit quietly and to each imagine what would make them feel safe. What did they need? One came up with a bright, shiny, new trashcan, complete with lid to be banged down at the first sign of trouble. A suit of armor was suggested as being more mobile, and a gale of laughter which blew away the fear, followed his comment that ghosts might know how to use can openers. Another chose a spacesuit—useful because he could see out and had a two-way radio to communicate. One had a kind of electrified cage, complete with cattle prod. Another had a shield and sword—rather like a *Star Trek* phaser in that it emitted pulses of laser energy. One of the girls hid in a crystal which had a little window to open if she wanted to reach out to the world; another was within an egg. Someone found herself in mummified form, protected by bandages of light wrapped around her. What fascinated me is just how universal these images are. These young people, who had no prior knowledge so far as they knew, had pulled, seemingly out of nowhere, several of the protective devices used down the ages in occult schools. (This is not so surprising if, like me, you believe in reincarnation.)

Once we had each one of them safely cocooned in their protection, I was able to talk to the entities who had been attracted by the Ouija board. This is not work for amateurs, and if you experience problems of this nature, it is important to call in an expert to help you. Your local Spiritualist Church will be able to advise if necessary but check that whoever does the work does actually direct the soul(s) on in their journey and not merely banish them from the place. (This simply leaves an even more angry and frustrated soul wandering about looking for someone else to latch on to.)

The effect on the punks was dramatic and instantaneous. All the depression lifted, the invasive thoughts stopped, and the nightmares ceased. Objects remained where they were meant to be. They went back to being a fairly normal group of teenagers. But they kept me on to teach them to meditate and two of the group eventually became healers. People who have strong psychic energy, of which they are unaware, do seem to stir up psychic activity around them. It can be a way of "attracting attention," of opening one's eyes to the fact that there is more on Earth than just the physical level, as well as alerting one to the need for psychic protection.

To clear the space in those days I used a meditation of passing light through the building, smudged with incense, blessed the place, and dedicated it to the highest spiritual energies. I also persuaded the young man who lived in the house to repaint his room some other color than matte black, and to remove the black shades from the windows, thus letting some natural light and air in (psychologically invigorating if nothing else). Nowadays, I would probably simply spray all around with Crystal Clear essence which is marvelous for cleansing crystals, rooms, people, anything. A few drops in water sprayed from a plant spray really does work wonders. I would also have the geopathic energies of the place checked out as certain geopathically stressed sites attract lost souls and facilitate psychic activity.

The Green Pyramid exercise which follows came from a hypnotherapist friend of mine. As I used it, it was adapted to meet various needs. I put wheels on the corners, for instance, so I could move around. A client found she needed a door to go in and out of. She had a massive pyramid protecting her house, another for herself and her dog, and a third for her car. When she was trying to cut the ties with a particularly persistent and depressed ex-lover, she experienced his invasive energy as sticky gray tentacles which tried to creep under the door. So, she electrified the outside of the pyramid and put a fence round it. After the tie cutting, we left the pyramid and fence in place. Later that day, a friend came to call and said, "What on earth have you been doing, I felt like I had to fight my way to the doorbell." It worked. The ex-lover stopped calling round on the pretext that, "I was just in the neighborhood and thought I'd see if you were all right."

When doing this exercise, it is important to remember that the floor goes under your feet, or under the building you are in. It is advisable to do the visualization morning and night for a few days, and then check from time to time that the pyramid is still in place. If you are doing the exercise at night, you can perform it lying down and let yourself fall asleep when it is complete.

⟩ The Green Pyramid

Settle yourself comfortably in a chair or lie in bed. Let yourself relax, breathing gently and establishing an easy rhythm. Let your eyelids lie softly, your hands fall comfortably in your lap. Gradually let the outside world slip away, bringing your attention deep into yourself.

When you are ready to begin, imagine yourself (or your room) surrounded by a translucent green pyramid. The pyramid is hollow and the sides are strong and firm. The base is below your feet, the apex above your head. Check that the sides are all there and meet the base firmly.

You are suspended within this pyramid, protected by its ancient energies. If you need to move around, then have wheels on the corners. If you need to see out, then have a window or door.

Spend a few minutes cocooned within this safe space. Enjoy the feeling you have there. Pyramids are powerful healing places. Allow the pyramid energies to neutralize any ill effects you have suffered from other people's thoughts or vibrations.

As you slowly bring your attention back into the room, remind yourself that this pyramid will stay with you; its protective force will be activated whenever it is needed. Nothing can penetrate through this pyramid unless you choose to allow it.

When you have completed the exercise, bring your attention fully back. Look around, recognize your surroundings. Be aware that the pyramid is around you, and then either get up and go about your daily life, or let yourself slip into sleep.

If you are non-visual: Make yourself a small model pyramid, or hold a pyramid-shaped stone. Explore it with your fingers until you know exactly the shape and feel of a pyramid. Allow yourself to sense this pyramid growing bigger and bigger until it is all around you (hollow, of course).

⚡ Meditation ⚡

MEDITATION IS A FORM OF SPIRITUAL COMMUNION. When we are able to still our everyday mind, we can contact the higher forces, lift our consciousness up to the spiritual realms. This contact may come as a moment of "bliss consciousness," a "deep inner peace and stillness," or a "sense of new knowing." We can also go deep within our self, contacting our subconscious energies or the divine energy within. As we have to open up our spiritual and psychic centers, we are vulnerable to intrusion from inner or outer sources. Having a clear intention, knowing our self well, and accessing a clear link with the highest levels all help our protection during meditation.

Always begin your meditation by strengthening your aura, activating its natural protection. Reach up to the highest possible spiritual vibration, actively seeking contact with your Higher Self and whatever name you put to the universal spiritual energy.

It is also necessary to pay attention to closing down afterwards. If we fail to shut down after meditation and to consciously ground our self in our body, then we are walking around wide open to invasion from inner or outer sources. Always complete your meditation by shutting down the chakras and checking that your grounding cord is in place. This grounding cord hooks deep into the earth, holding you in incarnation. Consciously take possession of your body again and place your feet firmly on the ground. Wrap a cloak of protection around yourself. You may like to stamp your foot firmly on the ground to reestablish your connection with the earth and signal that you are back in the everyday world.

The Findhorn Flower essence Clear Light has been specially formulated to bring about a peaceful state of mind and a mental clarity which aids meditation. "When heart, body and mind are still and aligned, a clear channel is created whereby the intuition, Higher Self and Higher (or Universal) Mind can be contacted." The Australian Bush essence Meditation has been formulated to "tap into the inner intelligence of the body, as well as providing auric protection, opening the intuitive and spiritual faculties, enhancing communication with the Higher Self. It includes Red Lily to open the crown chakra, at the same time remaining grounded, practical and earthed in your spirituality." Bush Iris opens the door to your higher perceptions and spirituality as well as clearing any blocks in the base, throat, third eye and crown chakra, enhancing trust. A few drops of either of these essences taken before meditation will enhance your protection. A combination of the Bush essences Fringed Violet and Flannel Flower will help you to close down again afterwards. If you find it difficult to stay still long enough to meditate, Black Eyed Susan helps you slow down and tune in to the calm still center within.

There are certain somewhat disturbing experiences which can occur when beginning meditation, but no-one seems to mention them beforehand. I am talking here about meditation as any process which reaches towards higher states of consciousness, regardless of the method. Some techniques will use mantras or the breath, trying to do away with thoughts and images; others will use images as a way in. Some might use sound, movement, stillness to calm and focus the mind, or to switch it off. We need to look at the mind pictures and experiences that may arise during this process. So often they are treated as garbage to be disposed of as quickly as possible, or as "outside interference" to be defended against, but these images can sometimes have value, as we shall see.

Some of the images are positive, but may not be perceived so at first, such as the eye that slowly opens and regards you unwinkingly (and who may well turn out to be an inner guide), or the hooded figure who stalks the edge of awareness. Other images are immediately present, and very frightening. The grotesque, leering faces that loom out from the mind's eye like computer graphics in the psychic mist. These faces also appear in the hypnagogic stages of sleep—just as you drop off or awake. This stage of sleep or meditation, is usually passed through quite quickly, but occasionally the faces linger, causing unease.

Such faces may form the basis of a bad trip for a drug taker who has no control as the contents of the subconscious mind rise to the surface. However, the meditator does have control over this subconscious "spring-cleaning" and can utilize the experience. Allowing the process to continue, consciously guiding its progress toward completion, maybe even replacing the faces with pleasant images, releases inner demons. Even when the faces have been cleared, vague fears or feelings of menace can linger and may need to be dispelled.

It is possible, of course, to rise rapidly through the lower levels of consciousness and so reach the higher levels where bliss or enlightenment can be found—the usual goal of meditation. As like attracts like, consciously reaching up to the higher levels takes you there. Nevertheless, it can be most productive not to pass too quickly through the lower levels but, by observing the process while not getting too caught up in it, to become familiar with the lesser known contents of consciousness and to embrace and reintegrate lost parts of our self. If we relax, slow down, let go of the controls, open up, they rise into consciousness as symbols, images or vague fears. We can then explore their origins and their usefulness. If they are inappropriate thought forms, we can wink them out of existence with the psychic laser. If they have value, we can work with them. It is these lost parts, lurking in the hidden recesses of our psyche that emerge to threaten us by their very existence. So, fully knowing our self is one of the best protections of all.

The human shadow is a psychologically validated experience. All the rejected and despised parts of our self that are "not nice," "not acceptable," "unclean," are pushed down out of sight, rejected, relegated to unconsciousness. All our negative emotional states such as guilt, unworthiness and shame attach themselves to the shadow, which lives in the subconscious mind along with forgotten memories and various characters from our past. Our shadow holds much of value. Unfortunately the "New Age" has relegated "the dark" to the clutches of "evil." Everything has to be light and bright, we have forgotten how to embrace the darkness. We have lost the balance of yin and yang. In our meditation we may need to sit in the darkness, like the germinating seed that sprouts best when there is no light. Meditation is an ideal time to nourish both our spiritual light and our darkness. We must not be too quick to rout out the darkness from our soul or its denizens. It is our ground of being. Nor must we always see it projected "out there" onto someone other, who is inevitably experienced as evil. Some forms of psychic attack come from these neglected and rejected parts of our self. They tend to rise up in meditation. It is the only way they can attract our attention. Often, they are those leering, grotesque faces.

❧ Face Clearing

As the faces rise up into consciousness, slow each one down and focus on one at a time. (This takes a little practice at first, visualizing a video remote control on pause can help.) Acknowledge the face. Accept it. Send it love. Bless it. Then allow it to go on its way. You may well find that, as you bless it, the face changes, becoming less grotesque.

In time a face may communicate with you. Ask what gift it has for you, what knowledge it brings, what rejected part of yourself wishes to return. Embrace that part, accept the gift, acknowledge your inner knowing.

If a face is particularly resistant and unpleasant, you can see it projected against a blackboard. Take an eraser, erase it piece by piece, replacing it with light. Or, switch the projector off and watch the image fade into blackness.

You can also replace the image with something more pleasant. Gradually replacing it with a beautiful flower built up petal by petal, or the picture of a beloved pet, changes the power that image holds. You will become adept at instantly transforming the grotesque into the beautiful—and eventually at recognizing the beauty in the grotesque.

If you are non-visual, you are unlikely to experience the faces but you may have a sense of unease or disquiet. Playing suitable music can help you to overcome this.

In meditation, we do not only have to face our own inner demons. The levels of being closest to the Earth, the astral plane, are divided by the thinnest of veils from the material world. As we raise our vibrations by lifting our consciousness to the spiritual, so we extend our consciousness into these realms. Our "spiritual light" shines out like a beacon. Various "undesirable elements" may be attracted to that light, just as evolved souls are drawn to us when we progress a little further into the spiritual realm. If we stay at the level of the astral plane, our insights, communications and so-called spiritual experiences may be anything but. Because they are, vibrationally, closest to us, it is the beings who inhabit these lower astral realms who can most easily communicate with us.

That "death is not an instant cure for ignorance" perhaps explains the confused, fanciful and downright weird nature of many psychic communications, especially channelings. This is not a new phenomenon. It has merely undergone a change of name. Years ago it was "the guides communicating." Before that, it was oracles from the gods. Common sense is your best protection in such circumstances, but aiming to raise your vibrations to the highest possible level will also bypass any possible hazards and ensure that your insights come from the highest possible source. If you do meet the less pleasant residents of these realms, then use the psychic phaser to protect yourself.

⟩ Cleansing the Subconscious Mind ⟨

SINCE MANY OF THE THREATS AND VAGUE fears we experience on the psychic level come from our own subconscious mind, the more we can cleanse this part of our being, the more protected we will be. Cleansing the subconscious mind does not mean even deeper repression of the "unacceptable" parts of our self and our involuntary terrors. It means letting go of all the things we are holding onto that we have outgrown. It entails meeting parts of our self that we are not aware of. It demands acceptance of our shadow qualities. It requires a recognition that, at a very profound level, we are all one.

Some of the work needs to be done during psychotherapy and deep introspection, but we can help the process by creative visualization and the use of flower essences and crystals. The Bush essence Billy Goat Plum helps to clear repressed feelings and self-loathing that arise out of sexual problems and discomfort with being in a physical body. Dagger Hakea helps you to resolve old feelings of resentment and bitterness, while Five Corners will help in cases of low self-esteem, bringing about love and acceptance of yourself. The FES remedy Chaparral clears psychic toxicity and Sunshine Wattle helps to release the part of you that is stuck in the past. These are excellent remedies to take before doing the following exercise. A dose of Crowea afterwards will help to realign your subtle bodies with the physical. A milky quartz crystal will help you get in touch with your subconscious mind, while an aquamarine helps to alleviate fears and phobias. You can hold a crystal while doing the following exercise.

Stay conscious of your body as you carry out the instructions. Not all the contents of the subconscious mind reside in your head. Many are stored in the muscles and skeletal system through your body. Your body has its own form of memory which needs to be honored.

❧ Exercise

Choosing a time when you will not be disturbed, settle yourself comfortably in a chair with your feet firmly on the floor. Take as long as you need to relax and become comfortable. Make a conscious connection to the chakra below your feet to keep yourself grounded. Breathe out any tension you may be feeling, especially any fear or anxiety you may notice coming up from time to time. See the anxiety leaving as a gray mist when you breathe out.

Be aware that there is a column of light all around you. But this is light with a difference. Light that is dark, warm, liquid, velvety. Allow this dark light to penetrate all the levels of your being. Draw it in through the top of your head until it fills the skull. Let it sink down through your brain, through the conscious mind and then deep into the subconscious mind. Let its velvety darkness fill every level.

Draw the dark light on down through your body, surrounding and interpenetrating each part, each organ, each fiber of your being, until it passes down through the chest, abdomen and legs to reach your toes.

Let your awareness follow this dark light. Let it reach down into the depths of the subconscious mind. Let it link into your emotional body through the solar plexus chakra. Open the depths of your being to this light.

Feel this dark light draw into itself all the toxic residue, imprints, old programs, outworn emotions, impurities, negative thoughts and feelings that are held there. Feel the gentle loving warmth of the dark delicately dissolving the places where disharmony and dis-ease lie. Surrender to the dark light all your fears, vulnerabilities, negative emotional states, unaccepted desires. All the blockages that your physical body has been holding onto which belong to the subconscious mind. Let there be no part of your being that the dark light does not know and love. Feel its healing touch on every level.

If thoughts, feelings, fears rise up into your conscious mind, acknowledge them without judgment, letting them dissolve into the darkness of the light.

Do not be afraid of experiencing yourself in your totality, dark and light, accepted and rejected, good and bad, known and unknown. Let the "dark light" help you to find the point of balance, the calm safe center around which all revolves in a ceaseless motion of yin and yang.

Sit in that safe place in the middle of the darkness. Feel how the liquid light flows through, bathing everything in its accepting luminescence. Take as much time as you need to complete this process...

Then allow the dark light to pass out through your feet into the welcoming earth below, taking with it all the toxic residues of your subconscious mind, leaving that mind cleansed, healed, and purified.

Seal the top of your head and below your feet with light, and then wrap a cloak of protection around yourself to seal your aura. Breathe a little more deeply, move around and bring your awareness fully back to your surroundings.

If you are non-visual: You do not need to see the light. Feel it moving through you. Chart its progress by the sensations in your body. Be aware of the energy changing and dissolving as the light flows through. Use your breath, breathe deep down into your belly. Then, as you empty your lungs completely, let any negativity flow out with your breath to dissipate harmlessly in the air.

❧ Meeting the Saboteur ❧

DESPITE OUR BEST EFFORTS AT GROWTH and evolution, we all harbor inner figures from our past. These figures may once have had a positive, protective role, but they have become fixed and rigid. They have been outgrown, but they cling tenaciously to life in the recesses of our psyche. One such ubiquitous figure is the saboteur, who arises to trip us up just as we are about to triumph. The saboteur feels, and behaves like, a very negative, critical, destructive person. And yet, when we are able to talk to him (it is usually a him but may be female or neuter), we find that he, in his eyes, has a good reason for his actions. It is just that that reason may not be appropriate anymore. Nevertheless, we can still learn from him, and maybe find him a more productive role in our lives. After all, his prime reason for existing is to protect us.

On a vibrational level, the Bush essence Five Corners helps to clear sabotage, so taking a dose before commencing this exercise is most beneficial. It should be followed up by two doses a day for two weeks or so.

❧ Exercise

Choosing a time when you will not be disturbed, settle yourself comfortably in a chair and let yourself relax and open. Keep your root chakra open to ground yourself and stay with your body.

When you are ready, picture yourself standing in front of an old house. Open the door and go in. Smell its slightly musty smell, see the dust lying all around. Explore its ancient rooms.

You will have to seek out your saboteur. He may well be lurking in the cellar, below the stairs, or in an attic room. Ask to be guided towards him.

When you find him, go into the room with him. He may be reluctant to speak at first, or may even be actively hostile. Have patience. Reassure him that you have come to listen to what he has to say. Ask him about his role in your life, how he came into being, what his function was, what you were doing at the time. Ask him how he believed he was helping you. You will find that, back in the beginning, there was a good reason for his actions (he was not always a saboteur) and that this may still be an area of life where you need some extra help and insight—where you may trip yourself up.

When you have learned all you can about how he came into being, explore how he now operates in your life. Investigate his part in your inner world. Does he have specific fears and concerns? Are they relevant today, or are they merely part of the past?

He will no doubt say that he is trying to keep you safe. Point out to him that, whereas he feels he is keeping you safe, he is actually sabotaging your efforts to evolve. He, and therefore part of you, may actually be afraid of growing. Find out what he needs before you can proceed. There may be something you are overlooking. What would make him, and you, feel safe? Ask him to cooperate with you, to remind you when you need to pay attention, but not to actively interfere without negotiation. If he has been hiding away in the basement or the attic, ask him where he would like to live. Help him to find a more comfortable space. Set up a signal so that he can gain your attention. Promise to visit, to keep the lines of communication open. Let him become an ally.

When you have completed the work with him, return your awareness to your surroundings. Wrap yourself in a cloak of protection and then move around the room.

If you are non-visual: Try having a dialogue with the saboteur. You can do this internally by listening for his voice: Try using two chairs. Sit on one as you speak to him and then move to the other chair as you listen to his response. Or do this externally by having two pieces of paper, one for your question, the other for his answer which will "just come" to you. (Again, you can use two chairs to aid the process.)

⸙ Channeling ⸙

CHANNELING, WHICH USED TO BE CALLED mediumship, has exploded in popularity over the last few years. With the result that many people, trained and untrained, are passing on messages from a variety of disincarnate sources. Many are attuned to frequencies beyond the normal reach of our earthly awareness. Some of these messages are of doom, others of hope; some are trivial, others very profound; some come from the Pleiades, others from Auntie Maud. All, to some extent or another, owe something to the mind of the person through which they pass: vocabulary, philosophical concepts, outlook, etc.

Therefore, the first precaution to take when channeling is to know the source. Is it the subconscious mind? (It frequently is, however cunningly disguised as highly evolved beings from beyond our solar system.) Is it wishful thinking, grandiosity, ego, lust? (An otherwise nondescript personality can gain great kudos from channeling an "evolved being." And, a surprising number of communicators advocate adulterous sexual union, usually with nubile young women or attractive men, "for the good of the planet" or "because you are soulmates and meant to be together." This may well be a case of telling someone what they want to hear but would not give themselves permission to do in other circumstances.) Does this being really have anything of value to pass on? (An awful lot of rubbish is spouted in the name of progress and evolution.) Are you in control, or does it control you?

One unfortunate family were under the delusion that they were receiving channelings, via "Greyhorse," from a high level of being. Greyhorse himself was said to be the spirit of a horse (which could in itself perhaps have raised a few questions). Unfortunately he always chose to "come through" just as a meal was being served, and everything had to stop while Greyhorse uttered his words of wisdom. The family endured many cold and congealed platters before one of my teachers happened to stay to supper. "What a lot of nonsense," she said, after a moment or two. Greyhorse left in a huff and did not return. The family had been duped by the pontifications of an astral joker.

The Australian Bush essence Angelsword helps you to distinguish between "good" and "bad" communication, and will repair your energy field if necessary. As its creator Ian White puts it, "It cuts out the crap." His Green Spider Orchid helps to convey spiritual information on many levels, and prevents too much spilling out when inappropriate.

Many of the pitfalls of channeling can be avoided by training in a properly organized, well-led development group. A group under an experienced leader who recognizes the problems and who teaches you to close down as well as open up, and who carefully monitors the quality of what comes through as well as watching for any signs of an overactive ego—or imagination. At this stage your best protection is someone else's experience— and your own common sense. As you progress, working within a group, no matter how small, ensures you always have someone there if you have any difficulties—and they can monitor the quality of the material and keep it on track. They can also make sure you can come back into your body when you've finished. If you are not the channeler, then you can use your common sense to assess what is being given to you.

It stands to reason that, if you are physically depleted, ill, emotionally disturbed, mentally unstable, or psychically unbalanced, you should not attempt channeling. Like attracts like. If you feel at a low ebb, a low vibration is what you will attract. If you are disturbed or unbalanced in any way, a disturbed or unbalanced communicator is what you will get—and there are plenty out there waiting for a chance. Equally, don't work if anyone else in the group is not up to par. Remember, a group works at the lowest common denominator.

If you do work alone, make sure you know who is communicating. Get to know your guides and guardian, and work with a doorkeeper to keep less desirable elements out. Doorkeepers have been around for a long, long time. In some traditions, everyone is allocated one at birth, much the same as a guardian angel. A doorkeeper's specific task is to watch over your body whenever your spirit leaves it: during sleep, out-of-the-body experiences, when working psychically, etc. The gatekeeper will also check the credentials of anyone wanting to psychically communicate with you, or to "borrow" your body or consciousness.

How much protection you need during channeling depends on how you work. Some people deliberately and completely "stand aside" from their body during the process. They allow the communicator to use their body's power of speech and sometimes movement too. They rarely remember what has been said. Obviously, at this level of trance work, you need to be very sure about who is temporarily "inhabiting" your body. You want to know that they are going to let your consciousness take over again. Some people work at a much lighter level. They consciously raise their vibrations so that the communicator telepathically passes the message on through the aura. This may be spoken or written, heard as an inner voice or received as an intuition. Any problems come when they are unable to close the link, when they cannot filter out the other consciousness from their own. And, when they cannot distinguish their own inner voices from disincarnate communication. The psychotic and the psychic are very close.

This is why mixing drugs and psychic work is unwise. Drugs, particularly hallucinogens, "blow the circuits" that protect from psychic overload. We all have natural protection mechanisms, "gates," that screen out unwanted psychic communication.

These natural barriers are our protection against invasion by something other. If these are blown open, and cannot be closed again, the mind is open to intrusion. Whatever the terminology, psychic training includes opening and closing these gates at will so that they remain under your control. In drug-induced or spontaneous psychic experiences, they do not.

The most important thing about channeling is to know how to close down again. This means it is under your control—and unwanted communication is kept out. Since channeling uses your energy field, deliberately lowering your vibration cuts off contact. Closing the chakras (physically covering the crown chakra if needed), making sure your grounding cord is in place and crystallizing the edge of your aura should do the trick. You will find that a hematite or bogie stone will ground you back into your body quickly but gently. If all else fails, picturing your doorkeeper yanking this unwanted intruder out of your psychic space usually works. It has to be a particularly insistent entity to resist all this. In which case a dose of FES essence Red Clover will complete the eviction. While channeling is taking place with your permission, do not let your consciousness stray too far and make sure you aim for the highest frequency possible. That way you can monitor what is going on and return your consciousness into your body if necessary.

❧ Meeting Your Doorkeeper

Settle yourself comfortably in a chair at a time when you will not be disturbed. Close your eyes. Spend a few moments relaxing and getting comfortable.

Then ask your doorkeeper to make him or herself known to you. Be alert for signals, a tap on the shoulder, a hand on your head, a tingling scalp, a pleasant perfume. You may see a clear picture, or you may strongly feel a loving protective presence with you. Allow plenty of time, do not force the process. Let your consciousness reach out to make contact and then be content to wait...

(You may need to do this several times before you sense the doorkeeper's presence. Making an appointment for a regular meeting at a certain time each day can be useful.)

If there is anything in the least scary in your supposed doorkeeper, if it is someone you know or have known, then ask them to leave and wait for your real doorkeeper to make themselves known. As this doorkeeper has been with you from birth, it is unlikely to be someone you have known in this life. (If someone from this life does appear, it may be necessary to cut the psychic ties, see page 93.) As they have been around you for a long time, they should feel familiar and comfortable even though an apparent stranger.

Take as long as you need to make close contact with your doorkeeper. Make any contracts you feel necessary about precautions and protection...

When you are ready to close, ask your doorkeeper to remain with you. Switch your attention back into the room. Check your cloak of protection is in place. Then get up and move around.

Practice calling on your doorkeeper from time to time before you need his or her services.

If you are non-visual: Hold one of the protective crystals (see page 126) in your hand for a few moments and ask that it will act as a doorkeeper for you. Then, whenever you meditate or raise your consciousness, hold the crystal in your hand and ask it to protect you.

⟩ Walk-Ins ⟨

ALONG WITH THE EXPLOSION IN CHANNELING has come a phenomenon known as "walk-ins"—the psychic equivalent of squatting in an unoccupied house. An alien being has taken over, or shares, a body with someone still attached to the earth but who has been only loosely connected to their physical body, leaving it open to the squatter. The reason for such loose connections may be drugs, too much meditation or trance work, "space-cadetting," lack of interest in the physical realm, psychiatric problems, choice, etc. Years ago this phenomenon was known as possession or obsession. According to the religious viewpoint of the observer, it was down to devils, lost souls, or the gods. Now, it is more likely to be put down to aliens from outerspace or highly evolved spiritual beings needing a temporary home on Earth. Whatever the source, it is a dangerous situation to find yourself in.

The only protection against a walk-in is to be fully grounded in your physical body. To live fully and physically in the present moment, ensuring that you completely close down your psychic centers after meditation or other psychic work, and especially after any form of channeling. Several of the flower essences can help to maintain the strong boundaries and grounding required (see page 119).

The cure lies outside the scope of this book as it needs professional help—see useful addresses (page 143).

Out-of-the-Body Experiences (OOBEs)

- "I was on the ceiling looking back at my body to which I seemed to be attached by a thin silver cord."

- "I fell out of bed and just kept falling. I went down through the ceiling and into the flat below. I picked myself up and started to explore. Eventually I walked back up the stairs and into my bedroom. To my surprise, I was lying on the bed."

- "I was flying through the air, I recognized the Thermos Factory and thought 'I'm nearly home now.' Then I was drifting back through my bedroom window towards my body which was lying on the bed, apparently asleep."

- "I was lying in bed beside my wife and was unable to get to sleep. I felt like a cigarette but they were down in the kitchen. So I got out of bed, went downstairs, through the living room and into the kitchen which was in darkness. When I tried to switch the light on, my fingers wouldn't operate the switch, which made me get very annoyed and a little worried. Suddenly, I found myself lying in bed next to my wife."

- "I suddenly realized I was in a strange place, walking among people I had never seen before. Although I seemed quite solid, I could walk through walls. I panicked and was yanked back. It was as though I was on the end of a fishing reel, being pulled in. To my great relief, with a big bump I landed in my chair and found myself sitting on my own lap. After a moment or two, I merged back into my body."

- "I met my grandmother who had died when I was a child. I put my arms round her and hugged her. 'Oh my little granny,' I said, realizing that I was now much taller than her. She had brought

my beloved German Shepherd with her. When I stroked my dog,
I could feel the nodules still in her coat. She was a strong and as
real as I was, although I knew my body was sitting in meditation
back at home."

These are accounts of a classic Out-of-the-Body Experience
(OOBE). Consciousness leaves the physical body behind and
goes wandering. It is housed in the etheric or astral body, a
much lighter vibration than the dense physical body. This
etheric body can pass through the seemingly solid objects of
Earth and travel vast distances. OOBEs are often spontaneous
but can be consciously induced. Padre Pio, an Italian monk
and healer, would appear to hundreds of people while his body
was elsewhere. A surprising number of "ghostly apparitions"
are of people still living. They are out of their physical body
and appear to relatives or friends, most often at night. Most
OOBEs occur when we are asleep, but some people can learn
to do it at will when awake. Many take place on the Earth
plane but some people travel to other realms, or different parts
of the solar system. A leading American researcher went to
one of the planets, some months before a space probe landed.
He brought back accurate and detailed information about the
previously unknown surface of the planet. Information that
was confirmed by the probe.

Recent revelations have confirmed that both America and
the USSR trained "psychic spies" who could travel, out of their
bodies, to a named target on "enemy" territory. They had the
advantage over spy satellites that they could go inside buildings
and report what they saw there. They may have been trained
for more active work too. During the Second World War there
was a "magical battle of Britain." Christine Hartley told me
how she, and others, would deliberately go out onto the astral
levels in order to fight Hitler's "magicians." This was much
more than the "positive thinking" used by some groups and the

mind battles carried on by others. Christine, a trained adept, was using magical working and psychic tools while out of her body, just as she "read" past lives by journeying back to the appropriate time. In the battle, she was literally fighting for her life, and that of millions of other people also. To Christine, OOBEs came naturally, she had always done it.

OOBEs are a feature of childhood. Most of my early memories are, when I recall them visually, seen from above. I am watching my body and my consciousness is not "down there." They also happen during shock or trauma, which is why so many "apparitions" are of living people, most often just at or around the point of death. When I was almost dying in childbirth, I found myself on the ceiling with a guide. I could clearly see myself on the bed. A nurse came in and said, "It's unusual to sleep through this stage of labor... Oh my god" and rushed off to get help. I was later able to tell the nurse the steps they had taken while I was unconscious.

OOBEs also tend to go hand in hand with psychic development. I had a spate of them when I began opening up. I remember being "rocked" backwards and forwards, quite hard, when I was meditating although my body did not move. Then, suddenly, I was looking down at my body. I found I could think myself to places, almost instantaneously. Physical distance made little difference. I would make psychic assignations with a friend, and we would compare notes by phone the next day. But I also found, as the experience progressed, that I was in places I would rather not be. The experience was not always entirely under my control. I seemed to be sent to places to observe, although I could "escape" if necessary. After a few months, the OOBEs no longer happened so regularly. I really missed them as I learned a great deal from those experiences.

OOBEs, or astral travel as it used to be known, are well documented; some accounts go back many years. Parapsychology researchers in the States, who have always been keen to "prove" these things, devised a test whereby they placed an object on a high cupboard in an adjacent room. The subject had to find the object, and report back on it. Many were successful. Other people simply had to "travel" wherever they could. One subject found himself in a kind of torture factory, not a pleasant place to be.

The ancient Egyptians believed we have a kind of "etheric double," the *ka*, which could leave the body during sleep or coma, and which could be commanded by other people. Around 800 B.C. a prince of Nubia summoned the ka of the Pharaoh to appear before his magicians in Nubia for punishment. The Pharaoh's own magician read out the summons, so the Pharaoh was well aware of it. The ka duly appeared in Nubia, where it was beaten 500 times with a stick. When the Pharaoh awoke the next morning, he had stick marks on his back. The power of the mind? Autosuggestion? Or had his ka obeyed the summons? The Prince of Nubia and his magicians clearly believed that they had punished the ka of their overlord "in a public place."

OOBEs also feature in Near Death Experiences (NDEs). An early account is from the Venerable Bede (A.D. 673-735), a Christian monk. His story is of "one among the Northumbrians, who arose from the dead, and related the things which he had seen, some exciting terror and others delight." The account does nicely illustrate the terrors which can await the unwary during an OOBE:

> We came to a vale of great breadth, on one side it appeared full of dreadful flames, the other side was no less horrid for violent hail and cold snow were flying on the other, both places were full of men's souls tossed from one side to the other. My guide said: "This is not the hell you imagine." When he had conducted me,

much frightened with that horrid spectacle, to the far-
ther end, on a sudden I saw the place begin to grow dark
and filled with darkness. When I came into it, the darkness, by degrees grew so thick that I could see nothing
besides it and the shape of him that led me... on a sudden there appeared frequent globes of black flames, rising as it were out of some great pit and falling back again
into the same...

I heard behind me the noise of a most hideous and
wretched lamentation, and at the same time a loud
laughing, as of a rude multitude insulting captured enemies. I observed a gang of evil spirits dragging the howl-
ing and lamenting souls of men into the midst of darkness. In the meantime, some of the dark spirits ascended
from the flaming abyss and beset me on all sides, and
much perplexed me with their glaring eyes and stinking
fire which proceed from their mouths... yet they durst not
touch me. Being thus on all sides enclosed with enemies
and darkness, there appeared behind me the brightness of
a star shining amidst the darkness, when it drew near all
those evil spirits dispersed and fled.

Books relating to the Tibetan Bardo (between life state)
recount much the same scene, as do many other commenta-
tors. It is a universal experience that crosses cultural boundaries over the eons. Courtesy of the Venerable Bede, we also
have a taste of the delights that many people experience during a NDE:

[His guide took him] into an area of clear light and a field
of fragrant flowers of delightful sweetness, with men in
white... I discovered before me a much more beautiful
light and so wonderful a fragrance proceeded from that
place. When I began to hope we would enter that

delightful place, my guide on a sudden stood still and then turning, led me back.

You will notice that, while they were clearly aware of their visitor, the "evil spirits" could not touch him. This is a very clear illustration of the "like attracts like" principle. As many people who have journeyed in this realm have found, if your vibrations are high enough, you will be protected. If you believe you will not be harmed, you won't be. The Venerable Bede's visitor had a guide with him, something you can call on if you do inadvertently find yourself in these realms. He was being shown this place for a purpose. When he "returned from the dead," he lived thereafter in a very different manner. He gave away his goods and entered a monastery in great contrition. This is a feature of NDEs. They change people's lives. So do OOBEs.

For many people an OOBE is exciting and challenging. It opens up possibilities, expands consciousness, gives you new levels to explore. You will never again feel limited by the perspective of earth. However, too much, or uncontrolled, astral traveling can cause a feeling of dissociation from the body and leave it open to walk-ins and psychic invasion. If you do go traveling astrally, it is as well to ask your doorkeeper to be extra vigilant until you get back, and to go properly equipped for traveling. Going "sky clad" is all very well, but a spacesuit or other protective gear is more appropriate. You may like to hold a fluorite crystal in your hand as you go; it acts as a psychic shield and aids astral travel.

If you find being out of your body an alarming experience, always remember that you can think yourself back. The simple command "Let me be back in my body" is sufficient. (Often the mere fact that you are frightened will automatically pull you back.) In esoteric literature, confirmed by many people's experience, we have a "silver cord" which maintains contact with our body. When this cord is severed, we die at the physical level. You can use this cord to get back into your body. Simply pull yourself along it, hand over hand, and you will come back to your body. Or, you can imagine your body has a fishing reel with you on the end. As the body reels you in, you return. A transporter is the space age answer to returning. Practice the command, "Beam me back, Scottie" a few times and you will then automatically return to your body.

If you find yourself wandering through rather grim realms, you can protect yourself with light and ask to be taken to the higher planes. Remember that like attracts like, so if you are fearful, you will be drawn to the less pleasant places; the Bush essence Dog Rose is the antidote to this. If you are troubled by negative thoughts, try placing a bloodstone on your forehead before you go traveling. It blocks out negative thoughts and cleans the energy. If you set your mind on positive and pleasant things, you are more likely to have a positive experience. If you find you have to stay in the lower realms, ask to be shown the lesson you are there to learn as quickly as possible. Ask your guardian to be with you for extra protection.

Vibrationally, Mouse Ear Chickweed, a Scottish Harebell remedy, helps you to feel safe when astral traveling. The Bush essences Crowea and Sundew realign your physical and astral bodies after an OOBE or a severe shock. The Bach remedy Clematis is excellent for those with a tendency to "space cadetting," being out of the body through ungroundedness, as are the Bush essences Red Lily and Sundew. They can protect against involuntary OOBEs. The herb St. John's Wort has always been used as a magical protector. You can burn it or use it as an essence. Either way, it will ensure a safe journey. If you feel "spacey" when you return, hematite or a bogie stone will gently ground you in your body once again, as will a smoky quartz crystal.

❧ Protecting Your Space ❧

IF YOU CREATE A SAFE SPACE IN WHICH to live, work or meditate, you will naturally have protection. Regular smudging, burning incense, drumming, rattling, spraying with Crystal Clear, etc., will keep the psychic air fresh and the vibrations clear. Flowers and plants are useful; spider plants in particular thrive on negativity but you need to position these carefully as, in *Feng Shui* terms, they "cut the *chi*" (energy). Large lumps of crystal also help to soak up bad vibes—but remember to cleanse them from time to time. Bloodstone and amber are useful as they clean as well as protect the atmosphere. A lump of black obsidian or quartz will absorb negative energies. If you want a cheap, easy to obtain protection, get a flint from the fields. It is worth spending a moment or two holding your crystal and asking that it will protect your space as this focuses the energy for you.

It makes sense to have your whole living space clear and protected, but you can pay special attention to the place where you meditate or do other spiritual work. Many mundane workspaces too could use a little extra help, especially as they tend to have fluorescent light and equipment that generates massive electromagnetic fields. No matter how good your personal protection, if you work in a place that has "bad vibes," in time you will become depleted and unable to maintain that protection. There are devices and flower essences to counteract electromagnetic fields. I find Yarrow Special Formula extremely good—it was formulated to neutralize the effects of the Chernobyl nuclear disaster. I always take a few drops whenever I sit down at the computer and then again whenever my energy flags. Few domestic computers or TVs are adequately screened. I was horrified when a meter was brought in to measure the fields generated by mine. In order to work in a space within the Health and Safety guidelines, I would need to sit ten feet away from it. Clearly impossible, so protection, physical and psychic is needed. I use a coil of copper wire wound around the lead as well as the Special Formula essence.

There is psychic contamination, too. Years ago when I first went to a healing group, I was fascinated to observe one of the healers "combing" her patient's aura with her hands. She then carefully carried whatever it was she had removed over to a corner of the room and dumped it. I had a mental picture of a psychic vacuum cleaner working away in that corner. "Oh no," she said "I leave all that to the guides." It seemed to me that the next person in the room would be open to picking it up again. To be on the safe side, I left a psychic vacuum cleaner plugged in and it is presumably still there but the hose is probably blocked by now. A little psychic maintenance is called for from time to time.

Many meditations teach a form of "de-stressing" where the chakras, or the emotions, or the aura, are cleansed and the contents dumped out. But, you need more than this. Something needs to transmute the energies or you will reabsorb them. (I always visualize putting them on a fire or washing them in running water.)

In a workshop I once saw one of the participants leap back as though from a very nasty smell. As I always create a safe space in which to work, I assumed it must be coming from one of the other participants. When the meditation was over, I asked her what had happened. "Well," she said, "It seemed to come from the lady next to me. All of a sudden there was this big black heap in front of me. It felt very nasty indeed. Remembering that the town had a huge bonfire in the square outside once a year, and knowing you always use fire to purify the energies, I hastily shoveled it outside and onto the bonfire."

When I asked the other woman what she had been doing, she said, "Oh, I wasn't getting anywhere so I decided to clean out my chakras." I queried what she did with the "rubbish." "I don't know," was the surprised response, "I just pull it out and dump it in front of me." She had been doing this for years, but of course as she did not transmute the energy, she absorbed it all back again—and wondered why she did not feel any better. Indeed, her health was deteriorating, which was why she had come to the workshop.

So, if you are doing any clearing or healing work, in addition to the space protection, you also need to put in place something to transmute it—crystal, light or fire—or to vacuum it up or otherwise disperse it safely. My "psychic vacuum cleaner" has an outlet in deep space. The contents of its dust bag get scattered harmlessly. If anything does reenter the atmosphere, it burns up.

If you are aware of any "bad vibes" directed towards your living space, a large mirror (physical) placed facing the direction they are coming from will direct them back to where they belong, as will jet, fluorite, black jade and other crystals.

There are several techniques you can use to create a safe space. Smudging with sagebrush is an ancient answer, spraying with Crystal Clear a modern one. The Green Pyramid exercise on page 52 is ideal as it gives all-round protection. The visualization for protecting group space (page 108) can be adapted and the barrier of light left in place. You might also like to program a protective crystal: rose quartz and amethyst placed together are most effective.

To provide extra protection when you meditate, you can also create an inner, and outer, temple to which you always go. Have a sacred space, no matter how small in which you keep an "altar" with crystals and sacred objects. You may like to include the statue of a protective deity. If you always use the same physical space, you will draw extra protection simply through the ritual of settling into a familiar spot that has had its vibrations raised by your previous spiritual work. You can also have the ritual of lighting a joss stick or a candle.

❧ To Create an Inner Temple

Picture yourself in a beautiful place, it can be by the side of a lake, in a forest, a meadow, on top of a hill. Whatever feels most appropriate for you. Really let yourself see this place. Feel the ground beneath your feet. Smell the perfumes of the air.

As you look around you will find a small, perfectly formed temple. Walk over to this temple. You will need to go up three steps to its gates. As you approach the gates will open. Go through and into the inner courtyard. Pass through the courtyard into the inner sanctuary. As you approach, the doors will open and you will see a place has been prepared for you. Settle yourself comfortably in this inner sanctum while you do your spiritual work or meditation...

When you are ready to leave, pass out through the doors of the sanctum which will close behind you. Move across the courtyard and out through the temple gates, which will silently close after you. Go down the three steps and walk back to your starting point.

This is the temple of your inner heart. Know that you can always return.

Bring your awareness back into the room and open your eyes. Ensure that your chakras are closed and your cloak of protection and grounding cord are in place.

❧ Space Clearing Tools ❧

❧ Smudging

You will need a smudge stick and a tin to put it in afterwards, or an incense burner or censer. A joss stick can also be used but less smoke is produced.

Light the smudge stick or incense. Once it is well alight, blow out the flame. It will smoke thickly. Using a feather, fan or hand, direct the smoke around the room, or around the person being smudged. Cover every corner, and the back and front of the person from head to toe. When you have finished, put it in a lidded tin to extinguish.

❧ Crystal Clear

Place a few drops of Crystal Clear in water in a plant spray. Set the spray to the finest mist possible. Spray all around the room holding the spray as high as you can. The droplets will fall to the ground, cleansing as they go.

Crystal Clear can also be used to clear people, crystals or talismans of any negative energies they have absorbed.

Crystal Clear is available from Petal Tone in England and is also available through Centergees in the USA if you are unable to get it at your local essence supplier (see useful addresses, pages 143 and 144).

❧ Rattling

While purpose made rattles can be used, anything that is available will substitute: a jar of dried beans, seeds or rice. Even a packet of cat biscuits can be used in an emergency. "Rattle" all around your body, each arm and leg. Pay particular attention to the chakras and to the back of the head. Then rattle all around the room, out to the farthest corners and as high and low as you can reach.

❧ Tibetan Bowls

Tibetan bowls can be played in one of two ways: struck with a beater or a stick continuously drawn around the rim. Either will quickly clear the energies in a room, particularly if you have spent a few moments communing with the bowl and asking it to clear the energies as appropriate. Turn with the bowl so that it faces all the directions in the room; circle it around and allow the sound to diminish naturally when appropriate.

⚡ Screening Out Other People ⚡

MANY OF THE PROBLEMS WE ENCOUNTER are from being too empathetic, too open to picking up emanations from other people. This is particularly so if you are a therapist, psychic or practitioner of complementary therapies. While it may be helpful at the time to feel in your body every ache, pain and emotional disharmony your client or patient is bringing, unless you are able to thoroughly clear this after the session, you will inevitably take some of that person away with you. Finding another way of tuning in to the same information can greatly assist your psychic health. Learning to listen to your intuition, "seeing" the information on your internal screen, is preferable to taking it into your body.

But you do not need to be a professional in order to pick up from those around you. Nor do you need to be in physical proximity. There are people who positively wallow in other people's emotional angst. They exude sympathy, that least helpful of states. The interest may hold a destructive charge for both parties. Rarely does the local gossip realize just how much she is picking up from those she talks about with such intense interest. There are people who act like a sponge, soaking up atmospheres and psychic effluent. Their auras are none too strong. Their boundaries are elastic, their feelers everywhere. Indeed, psychics sometimes describe such people's auras as "leaking like a sieve" (Fringed Violet is the remedy for this).

Other people may have "blown" their protection through drugs, illness, geopathic stress, or unwise psychic experiences, or simply because they do not pay attention to protecting their auras. Certain people are naturally more absorbent and empa-thetic. The astrological water signs (Cancer, Scorpio, and Pisces) are especially prone to this although Cancer and Scorpio tend to protect themselves by instinct. But other signs too can have the particular planetary combinations or rising sign that indicate a "leaky aura," and even the most practical and pragmatic of signs may have something in the astrological chart which will cause unexpected vulnerability. Consulting an astrologer will tell you in which areas you are open to psychic invasion and can also pinpoint the people around you who will hook into this vulnerability.

A friend of mine found herself feeling anxious, panicky and infinitely sad. She recognized these as feelings she had had about twenty-five years ago when her father was dying. She had been doing a great deal of work on letting go the past and had allowed the feelings to come up so that she could release them. But, at the same time, one of her friends, whom she had not seen for sometime, was strongly on her mind. When she managed to contact him, he had just returned from his father's funeral. She knew from their astrological connections that she did interact with him strongly on a psychic level, without being physically close, but had never had quite such a graphic illustration of "feeling his feelings" before. It was quite difficult for her to sort out just how much of it was his, and how much was her own unresolved issues over her father's death. His experience was picking up on, and heightening, her own. When we looked at the charts, we were able to clarify how this process came about and this enabled her to focus on her own issues more clearly. At the same time, she was able to offer him support based on her own experiences: true empathy rather than sympathy.

Having such precise information means you can target your protection more effectively. You may need to cut the ties, especially at the chakras, if someone is draining you or if you are picking up too much telepathically. You may also need to step up your protection around certain people, especially if they are experts at pressing your emotional buttons. Being too defended all the time takes enormous energy, so it is good to know too whom you can relax with and be open to in safety.

You do not necessarily have to be too open at the auric level to suffer depletion. Simply sharing a bed with someone with whom you are energetically incompatible may lead to you waking up feeling tired and drained. Spending too long in the company of someone with a very different energy balance can also devitalize you. Those same astrological elements that indicate "weak" or "strong" boundaries, also have a great deal to say about your energy levels and who will "feed" or "drain" that energy. Generally speaking, people with the same element balance as you will feed your energy whereas someone with the opposite element balance may drain it. At its most super-ficial level, someone with the Sun in Pisces, for instance, could be fed by another water sign, Scorpio or Cancer; but drained by the fire signs, Aries, Leo and Sagittarius because fire superheats water into steam which dissipates. This is not a simple matter, however. For a short time, the Pisces could feel highly energized by the hot energy of the fire sign. But, eventually the "circuits would blow" and the energy disappear, Pisces is not energetically attuned to handle that much heat. In the initial stages, the Aries could feel devitalized by the cool water sign: it takes a lot of energy to heat water. But, when the steam was dissipating, the hot energy would feed Aries and drain Pisces.

The situation is further complicated by the position of the planets in your chart. You might have a water sun sign, but the other nine planets could be placed in fire and air. In which case, you would be much more at home with Aries, Gemini, Leo, Virgo, Sagittarius and Aquarius. Other element imbal-ances are equally likely. Fortunately, an astrologer can point all this out to you in a few moments. The astrologer can also look at someone else's energy balance and tell you whether this is compatible with yours, or not.

If the energy balances are not compatible, all is not lost. Divorce is not inevitable, although you may need to alter your sleeping arrangements. The problem is often solved quite simply by having separate beds. If the depletion is too severe, then separate rooms may be needed. You can rearrange other relationships too. See friends for shorter visits if you find their energies overpowering, or step up your protection for the duration. If it is your boss or a colleague who is draining you, plenty of plants and appropriate crystals can help to form a physical and psychic shield—spray them regularly with Crystal Clear. You can also mentally pop the person causing the problem under a glass bell jar as added protection and, of course, remember to activate your own shield each morning before work.

There are practical ways you can protect yourself from picking up from other people (hands over the solar plexus for instance), and there are essences to help you do this. You can wear jet, tiger's eye or turquoise. But the best protection of all is one that is in place all the time: a strong aura (see page 4) with its psychic shield. When you wake up, ensure your protection is in place; check it during the day and last thing at night. Even though it will become automatic, you still need to pay attention to it. If you need to pick up information, then your protection should include something like a two-way phone or a video screen so that you can see or hear the problems without having to experience them in your body. Standing under a shower (real or visualized) will help to wash away any residue afterwards, and Crystal Clear sprayed around the room and yourself will complete the cleansing.

The Gem Remedy Association make an Auric Protection remedy especially for therapists and those who are too sensitive to other people's emanations. The Bush essence Angelsword repairs "leaky auras," knitting together the energy field as does Fringed Violet. The Bach remedy Centaury is for people who are easily put upon and lack boundaries, while Mountain Pennyroyal will prevent taking on negative thoughts from others and Walnut will offset an over-susceptibility to the influence of others. Yarrow forms a psychic shield against bombardment by other people's feelings and needs, and Golden Rod (FES essence) gives you strength to retain your individuality despite pressure. The Desert Alchemy essence Wild Grape prevents enmeshment of your boundaries with someone else's.

❧ The Psychic Screen

Picture yourself surrounded by a screen of light at the outer edges of your aura. It completely covers you, going over your head and under your feet. This screen automatically filters what you pick up from other people. It filters out negativity, dis-ease, bad vibes, anger, fear and anything else that may harm you. Keep that screen in place whenever it is needed.

If you need to be aware of what people are thinking or feeling, the screen should incorporate a video screen with sound facilities. Then you can be shown all you need to know on the video. If necessary, have a two-way telephone so that you can ask questions.

If you are non-visual: Wear a piece of fluorite or other appropriate crystal and ask that it will enhance your psychic screen.

⸙ Psychic Protection and Children ⸙

WHILE WE CANNOT FULLY PROTECT SOMEONE else, if they are young, weak or vulnerable, we can boost their protection through prayer, visualization or flower essences, etc. This is particularly important if you have children around as they tend to be much more open psychically. They are still naturally in touch with other levels of being, particularly until they go to school. They are attuned to the energies of a place too, and so vulnerable to geopathic stress. They are in touch telepathically with all that goes on around them, absorbing like a psychic sponge the thoughts, feelings and emotions of adults.

As these are often at odds with what adults tell them is going on, they can become confused and bewildered, resulting in a "disturbed child." The confusion is compounded by adults telling them they are "being silly" or "making it up" when, in all innocence, they recount stories of the friends, or enemies, they have met on the other levels of being, or when they reflect back what they are picking up on the emotional and psychic level. If you are constantly put down, or worse still smacked, for "such nonsense," your natural inclination is to shut off. This works with most children, psychic ability is repressed, forgotten about. But it doesn't work with all children, the most sensitive can still feel this other world, and the unspoken thoughts around them. They often feel guilty, as though it is all their fault: children believe they are omnipotent. If they "see" that someone is ill or is going to die and then it happens, they feel that they have caused it. If their parent is emotionally upset, they believe they are responsible.

A disturbed child has ruffled psychic energies that can attract psychic disturbance—a vicious circle that can lead, especially at adolescence, to poltergeist activity, schizophrenia and hauntings. The Bush essences Fringed Violet, Red Helmet Orchid and Sundew can greatly help such children. Yarrow can provide a psychic shield for the child who picks up too much of the thoughts and feelings of others. While Dog Rose is excellent for nightmares, Sundew will bring the child who lives perpetually in a dream world into the everyday world.

It is always worth being honest with children, to the extent that they are capable of understanding—which should not be under-estimated. Mothers who deny that they are upset when the child is clearly aware of that upset is pointless—and leads to a situation where the child cannot trust his or her perceptions. Similarly, listening to a child who recounts a psychic experience should be done with love and respect. You don't need to pretend that you can see something too, but you do need to validate the child's experience by saying "Yes, I believe you" and letting them talk, especially if they are afraid. An adult matter-of-factly accepting what they say is calming and, contrary to popular opinion, does not lead to an overdeveloped imagination. (This, and nightmares, are most likely to arise from suppressed psychic awareness.) In this way, children learn to trust their psychic perceptions and intuitions. As being in touch with your own inner guidance, which develops out of perception and intuition, is a powerful protection, you are helping them to develop their own defenses. The Bush essences Sundew and Little Flannel Flower help children to have clearer contact with their spiritual guides, as well as helping to ground them in their body.

You can get children to draw their experiences, or write them as a story. Sometimes their perceptions and precognitions show up in spontaneous drawings. My six-year-old grand-daughter got up one morning and drew a family friend. She was all in black, with black chakras joined by a jagged line, and a big black cloud above pouring rain down. This was most unlike her usual colorful pictures. By that afternoon, the bottom had fallen out of the friend's world. She was emotionally devastated and in shock. A "black cloud" of depression hung over her. The picture was of a prophetic dream. As soon as she saw her, my granddaughter had her precognition confirmed. But she also needed to know that she had not caused this—a common misapprehension among young (and not so young) psychics.

Children delight in games, so visualizations of placing a brightly colored balloon of light around them, or of jumping into a bright shiny new trashcan for protection, are seen as fun. They also believe in the potent power of objects, so dream catchers work well to prevent nightmares. Crystals and furry animals are comforting. And generations of children went to bed protected by a prayer and a picture of Jesus watching over them. Many still do.

You can also utilize children's psychic abilities to talk to them while they sleep. It is not necessary to be physically present as distance makes no difference. This is an opportunity to reassure them, to explain things, or to simply send them love and healing.

All you need to do is to sit quietly, close your eyes and picture them. See yourself linked by a golden thread from heart to heart, third eye to third eye. Open your heart, allow the words to form in your mind and let them flow, with love. When you have finished, disengage the golden threads, leaving light to seal the places where they touched each of you. You may like to finish by seeing the child surrounded by light.

Do not be tempted to use this technique as a means of imposing control on a child. By all means ask them for cooperation in what you would like to achieve, but do not use mental force. This would be a psychic attack that removes free will, and the consequences will come back to you with renewed force.

⟩ Strengthening Another Person's Aura ⟨

ONCE THIS EXERCISE HAS BEEN PRACTICED a few times, it can be done in moments. As you are not using your own energy, it will not deplete you in any way, nor will it establish psychic connections between the two of you. If there is any doubt or possibility that psychic ties may be binding you, then the tie-cutting exercise on page 102 should be carried out first.

This is an exercise that must only be carried out with the best and most disinterested of motives. If you are looking, even unconsciously towards gratitude or control, or seeking to bind the person to you, your actions will constitute a psychic attack. So be perfectly clear and honest with yourself about your intentions before you begin.

⟩ Exercise

Choosing a time when you will not be disturbed, seat yourself in a quiet place. Close your eyes and focus your attention inward.

On your inner screen, picture the person whose aura you would like to see strengthened. Visualize a column of golden spiritual light surrounding and enclosing their aura. Let this golden light form a cloak of protection around them.

If you do happen to notice a cord tying you together, use a pair of golden scissors to snip it free and let the light heal where it has been.

When the exercise is complete, let the image fade into the distance so that the person moves out of your psychic space and goes back to their own space.

Check that your cloak of protection is in place before bringing your attention back into the room.

The following is particularly good if you are nonvisual, but it is highly effective in any case:

Place a photograph of the person face down with the crystal on top. I am always careful to insure that the crystal does not actually sit on top of the person if I am strengthening psychic protection. I place it adjacent to, but not on, the body so that it touches the aura. I like to use amethyst, clear or rose quartz crystals, but you can use a favorite crystal or select something appropriate. In cases of severe psychic attack, I have successfully used a black tourmaline.

Appropriate Flower essences should be added to spring water and stored in a dropper bottle. Place 7 drops on the crystal 2 or 3 times a day. Petal Tone Essences, which work through the aura and chakras, are particularly good when used in this way.

⁊ Tie Cutting ⁊

THERE IS A MARVELOUS DESCRIPTION BY George Ritchie (in *Return from Tomorrow**) of a tall, strong, highly successful son happily pursuing his business and social life. Next to him, hanging onto his coat sleeve and nagging incessantly, is his mother. She is dead, but has not realized this. She is unable to let go. He is seemingly oblivious to her presence, but every so often he absentmindedly brushes his sleeve. At a subliminal level, he knows she is there. Her opinion of him still motivates much of what he does.

The incident was seen during a Near Death Experience in which the observer, George Ritche, was taken on a tour of the realms nearest to the Earth. It vividly illustrates just how close the Earth and the astral planes are and how they interact. The mother was able to see, and touch, her son. However, mothers, and other people, do not need to be dead to hold on in this way. Wherever there are strong emotions, we hold onto or are held by the object of those feelings. We speak of "having her claws into him," of "being hooked," of "cold shouldering." Someone in love feels, "he is part of me." So often love equals enmeshment. A lost lover may be "in my head all the time." "I feel part of me has gone with her." I have heard a mother say of her child, "she is so gorgeous I could eat her." The bonds so created may be positive or negative. All leave their psychic mark. All enable someone other to reach into us. Once we become aware of these possibilities, we may find that we have been sharing our space with some

---

*George G. Ritche, *Return from Tomorrow* (Tarrytown, NY: Revell, 1988).

unexpected people: teachers, employers, long-dead relatives, old friends with whom we have lost touch, ancient enemies we had forgotten. It is not just our family who have a hold over us, although as theirs was the first, it may be the strongest.

With our inner eye we can "see" what binds us. The ties may appear as hooks, nets, cables, tree trunks and many other variations linking us inextricably to the other person. The ties seem to be indissoluble, but they are not. They appear that way only so long as we allow the other person to have a hold over us, which means we can cut our self free to be our own self once more. We can regain our autonomy. The work involves cutting the emotional and psychic ties and expectations that have built up. It does not cut off unconditional love, but it does remove the conditions, the oughts, shoulds, buts and "if-onlies" that can masquerade as love. Unfortunately, so often "love" is a means of control. A subtle radiation of acceptance or non-acceptance based on what the other person believes to be "best." In conforming, we lose our self. In losing our self, we are open to abuse and infiltration. Without strong protection, we may give a small piece of our self away to a comparative stranger in anger, passion or sympathy. Lacking awareness of our boundaries, we may have no resistance to the "psychic vampire" who hooks into our energy system and drains us. In the name of "love" we may allow a parent or partner to abuse and misuse us. Other more subtle abuses stem from different sources: our upbringing, religion, society's expectations, our spiritual training. (Many gurus are on a power trip—no matter how cunningly this may be disguised—and the church has a powerful hold over those it purports to be "saving.")

Tie cutting is powerful work. It should only be undertaken if you feel it is right for you. Any lingering doubts or ambivalence should be dealt with first. If you feel you owe someone something, you probably need more than most to cut the ties. Guilt is disempowering, and highly abusive on both sides. The

same applies if you feel responsible for someone. (It he.
remember that we can only ultimately be responsible for ᵥ
self.) Any conflicting emotions should be separated out. If you
are confusing love with support, support with collusion, collusion with responsibility; then, not only are you open to invasion by that person, but the underlying ambiguities will prevent
you from fully cutting the ties.

Over the years I have learned many different ways of cutting
the ties. One of the simplest is to picture the other person and
say firmly, "I take back all that is mine. I give back all that is
yours" and let them go in love. Many techniques have been
"given" to me when I needed them during work with a client;
that is, they just popped into my mind and were exactly right
for that particular person. Not surprisingly, many other people
use the same methods. Years ago when I did tie cutting people
would say: "Oh, you must have read Phyllis Krystal's book." I
hadn't, but when I attended one of her workshops I could see
the similarities.* Years later a German practitioner complained
bitterly to me that she had stolen his idea. We had all plucked
the idea "out of the air" (in their case via a guru) at about the
same time. I am a great believer in the cosmos supplying what
is needed, if only we stop to listen. No one can say "this is
mine, I had this idea first." Such tools have always existed.

My first introduction to tie cutting came from Christine
Hartley who had been practicing it for fifty years. She envis-
aged a tie linking the two navels (like a psychic umbilical
cord). She then had a pair of large, gold scissors, with which
she snipped the cord. She also used a hoop of light which could
be pulled up for immediate cutting and protection. I found
that, using these methods, there was a need for something
extra. A healing and sealing of the place where the ties had

---

* Phyllis Krystal, *Cutting the Ties that Bind* (York Beach, ME: Samuel Weiser,
Inc., 1993).

been. I used healing light for this. I also became aware that people needed to have their space protected while doing the work. So, I created circles of light for them to work in. When I realized that the ties presented themselves in many ways, I found that a variety of tools were required to remove them, but always the need for healing remained.

The mind is such a powerful tool. If you, in imagery, remove something from the body without healing the place, it may well manifest physically. This is even more likely if the tie cutting is only partial. The example I always use, because it is the most graphic I have ever seen, is the woman who had an adult drug-addicted son with whom she was inextricably enmeshed and with whom she unconsciously colluded—buying his heroin, for instance, and giving it to him in decreasing doses in order to "wean him off." The son, of course, simply supplemented his mother's dose from his own sources. He did not only take her resources in the form of cash. She felt responsible for his addiction because of her, and his, bad relationship with his father. She was utterly drained of energy by her attempt to "save him" and yet she continued to give him her all. When she attended a Phyllis Krystal workshop, she was ambivalent about cutting the ties with her son because, deep down, she believed that in cutting the ties she would cut off the support she felt he need-ed from her (a good example of confusing love with support, and also of not being in touch with her true feelings. She very much needed him to need her). It was a case of her head say-ing one thing—intellectually she understood the need for the cutting to set him free to be his own person—but her heart say-ing something else: "He is my responsibility." She "fell asleep" during the cutting, but told no one. She had seen the tie with her son as a tree trunk linking their navels, and had used a scalpel to remove a small part of it. A few days later she came to me. Her navel was raw and bleeding. When she told me what had happened, we completed the cutting. It took several hours and a great deal of work but in the end she was able to let him go in unconditional love. After the cutting, she slept for twelve hours during which time her navel healed. Her son then went into successful treatment of his own accord.

This often happens. In cutting the ties, the energy changes. People's lives then change for the better. Tie cutting restores not only our autonomy but our psychic energy. We can create better lives for ourselves, and we set the other person free to do the same for themselves. All relationships benefit from tie cutting. No matter how loving a relationship, expectations build up, oughts and shoulds creep in. Regular clearing of these aids a healthy relationship to thrive, and may even heal an ailing one. As part of your protection program, examine all your relationships to see if they would benefit from energy clearing in this way. We extend so much of our energy to the people with whom we are enmeshed without our recognizing it, that it makes sense to regularly clear our ties.

When I was under psychic attack, I realized that a great deal of the energy being thrown at me was actually coming from me, or rather from where I live, which is on a powerful healing Earth energy line. The person concerned had done a great deal of psychic development with me. He was "plugged into" the energies I used. After cutting the ties with him, I pulled out the plug linking him into the energies. He went down like a spent balloon. To prevent the link from being reestablished, I used a tube of light to protect myself, and from time to time I would hose both of us down with a laser light.

Having done tie cutting for over twenty years now, I find I can use short cuts, like the laser light or simply putting myself on a mental bonfire and asking for all the ties to be removed while my energies regenerate. Once you have established the basic principles, you may well find yourselves doing the same. Crystallizing the outer edge of your aura will also help to avoid reestablishing the bonds.

The tie cutting exercise which follows is, in my experience, the one that people find the easiest to do unaided. It is best done alone as a visualization, as having the other person physically present can prevent the cutting. You should not let the circles overlap (peg them down if necessary). It is surprising how far you can reach from the protection of your circle, and you can always ask for a guide to assist you if you have any difficulty. The meditation is set in a meadow but some people find it easier to picture the seashore, the side of a lake, or some other peaceful place. It is important to use your own images, rather than ones I impose on you, so adapt the wording if necessary.

During the imaging work the ties can manifest in many ways—as nets, hooks, umbilical cords, etc.—and in many places. It is quite common to find a sexual tie linking you to a father, sister, brother or mother. These images are the subconscious mind's way of symbolically representing an emotional truth and should be accepted as such. Part of the work involves removing the ties, the place where they have been on each person being healed and sealed with light. The other part involves destroying them. I find the most useful way of doing this is to have a large fire, as again the symbolism is important. As the fire burns, it transmutes the tie into energy. It is also possible to use water to dissolve or wash away the ties. The one method I do not recommend is to bury them, as symbolically this does not free you from them, and they may well sprout and grow again. Having said that, I have learned from years of experience that it is impossible to be dogmatic as, just occasionally, a tie may be transformed through death and rebirth, of which the ritual of burying can be a part.

If you have difficulty imaging the actual person, especially if they have been long dead or if you are particularly afraid of them, then put a photograph in the circle and work with that. It can be useful to do a blank cutting; that is, put the circle in place and ask for the most appropriate person with whom to cut the ties to appear. It can throw unexpected light on old ties that are leaving you vulnerable.

When working, cut the ties from your self first, remembering to heal and seal each place with light as you work. Then, if you do happen to "fall asleep" you will be protected. Transmuting the ties, by burning or whatever method you choose, releases all your creative and psychic energy that has been held by those ties. You will feel reenergized and much stronger in your self.

A dose of the Bach remedy Walnut will greatly aid you in tie cutting. (It can be taken for several days beforehand if you feel the cutting will be troublesome.) The Bush essence Dagger Hakea will help you with the forgiveness stage if this proves difficult or painful. Spraying your self with Crystal Clear also helps cut the ties.

ϟ Tie Cutting Visualization

Let your self relax and open to this work. Imagine your self standing in a beautiful meadow on a warm sunny day with just a gentle breeze playing around you to keep you cool and comfortable. Let your self feel the grass underneath your feet. Experience how it tickles your toes. Smell the air around you.

Spend a little time exploring your meadow and then choose the spot where you want to do this work. You will need a large flat area where you can have a bonfire, running water if you would like it, and anything else you will need.

Draw a circle around yourself as you stand in the meadow. The circle should be at arms length and go right around you. You can use paint, chalk, light or whatever comes to mind. This circle delineates your space.

In front of you, close to but not touching, draw another circle the same size, and picture the person with whom you wish to cut the ties inside it. (If you have difficulty in seeing the person clearly, you can picture a photograph being placed in the circle.)

Explain to the person why you are doing this exercise, tell them that you are not cutting off any unconditional love there may be, but that you wish to be free from the old emotional conditioning and psychic bonds that built up in the past, and any expectations in the present.

Look to see how the ties symbolically manifest themselves.

Then spend time removing them, first from your self, healing and sealing the places where they were with light; then removing them from the other person. Make sure you get all the ties, especially the ones around the back which you may overlook. Pile the ties up outside the circle. Wrap healing light around your self and the other person.

When you are sure you have cleared all the ties, and sealed all the places where they have been, let unconditional love, forgiveness and acceptance (where possible) flow between you and the other person.

Then move that other person back to their own space, out of your inner space. Let them go to where they belong in their own space.

[Repeat the cutting with another person if you wish or do a blank cutting to see who appears in the circle in front of yours.]

Then, gather up all the ties and find an appropriate way of destroying them. You may wish to have a large bonfire onto which you throw them, or a swiftly flowing river into which you cast them. Make sure you have destroyed all the ties.

If you are using a fire, move nearer to the flames and feel the transmuted energy warming, purifying, healing and energizing you; filling all the empty spaces left by removing the ties. Absorb as much of this energy as you need. If you feel able to, move into the fire and become like the phoenix, reborn from the flames. Wrap light around your self as protection.

If you are using water, you may like to enter the water to gently wash away the residue. Use the heat of the sun to purify, heal and energize your self, and then form a cloak of protection afterwards.

When you have completed all the cutting you wish to do, bring your attention back into the room and allow your self plenty of time to readjust, breathing more deeply and bringing your self into full awareness. Check that your cloak of protection is in place and that your aura is intact. Ground your self by hooking your grounding cord deep into the earth. Then get up and move about.

If you are non-visual: Drop Crystal Clear, or Walnut, essence onto a crystal placed on the photograph of the person with whom you wish to cut the ties. Say firmly, "I take back all that is mine. I give back all that is yours." Repeat this procedure twice a day for a few days. When you have finished, burn the photograph.

You can also use Crystal Clear essence in your bath water, asking that the links between you and the other person be cleansed or severed.

Note: If you have letters, photographs, jewelry, clothes, ornaments, etc., belonging to the other person, and particularly in cases where you know you are being harmed by their energies, you can burn the letters or photos. Pass clothes onto a charity shop. Cleanse jewelry and ornaments with Crystal Clear or better still have a yard sale and clear your attachment to any of the objects linked to that person. Use the money to buy yourself something you really like, a crystal or a piece of jewelry that means something to you and which will symbolize your new freedom.

So often the ties we have with other people come about through "love" relationships. Sexual contact can leave us tied to even the most casual acquaintance. But other chakras can be affected by our contacts. Some people "hook into" a particular chakra, which may link to an old problem. Sexual chakras are obvious, throat problems not so obvious: they relate to someone who stifled our ability to communicate, to speak our truth. The heart chakra links to someone who affected our ability to love openly and unconditionally. Our crown chakra may be blocked by someone with whom we, seemingly, had a spiritual contact but whose ego is holding us back. So it is worth checking our chakras to see if we have any unwanted ties still in place:

❧ Chakra Tie Cutting

Picture your self standing against a white background. If you feel the need, place your self in a circle of light for protection. Now have the other person come to stand next to you.

Using your inner eye, check the ties between each of the chakras in turn on you and the other person. Clear and heal both chakras with a whirlpool of light after you have removed any hooks or ties. Then move on to the next pair.

When all the chakras are clear, let the other person go on their way with your unconditional love.

If you are non-visual: You can use a pendulum to check for any chakra links while you think about the other person. Appropriate crystals can be used to clear any blockages. Rose quartz, for instance, is most suitable for the heart. Azurite works well on the throat and moldavite on the third eye. A Herkimer diamond, on the other hand, will clear any chakra although it should be used with caution on the third eye or crown chakras as it is extremely powerful in these areas.

❦ Group Protection ❧

GROUPS TEND TO ASSUME THAT, SIMPLY because they are oriented towards spiritual work, they will naturally be protected.
Sadly, this is not the case.

There are several ways in which the group is particularly
vulnerable:

- *Jealousy from outside the group;*
- *Jealousy from within the group;*
- *Disharmony within the group;*
- *Egotism and power struggles;*
- *Lack of proper guidance;*
- *Ignorance—not knowing what they are doing;*
- *Attracting the wrong kind of interest;*
- *Using an unsafe place;*
- *The purpose of the group itself;*
- *What the individual members bring to the group;*
- *Groups operate at the lowest common spiritual denominator.*

How a group comes together, what its motives are, and how
the group interacts are extremely relevant to how safe it feels
for its members.

As a novice, I was once part of a large, church-sponsored,
development group. It contained 25 people, all at different levels
of knowledge, understanding and ability. The group purpose
was spiritual development although in actuality, the focus was
on "giving messages" to each other. The setting was a

Spiritualist church, to which many souls were drawn back for communication and where they then lingered rather than going on their way once more. Nothing was ever done to clear this.

The group were disharmonious to say the least. One couple, a husband and wife, wanted to split up but were financially tied. They communicated only through a third party. Neither would give up attending the circle, nor would the leader ask them to leave. They sat opposite each other, and glowered. The undercurrents were lethal. Another couple were having an affair. He would not leave his wife. She was jealous and resentful. He felt guilty. To make matters worse, another member of the group made it clear that she strongly fancied him. One member had psychiatric problems, being schizophrenic and deeply disturbed (he was later, supposedly, taken over by an "evil entity") another dabbled in hard drugs. One recently bereaved woman was a brilliant psychic, much envied by several members, but totally ungrounded and emotionally bereft. Married, she had an affair with three of the younger men in turn. To cap it all, the leader was a closet gay who made covert advances to those same young men. It was a hotbed of intrigue and conflicting emotions, a most unsafe place to be. People came, and went, at random.

But at 7:30 on a Thursday evening, following a quick prayer, everyone sat down to meditate and were supposed to be in perfect harmony. Clairvoyant messages were then "given off," some bitchy in the extreme—as might have been expected. Many of the members were not destined to be conventionally clairvoyant. I "saw" past lives. "No such thing" said the leader. Others received spiritual philosophy, healing diagnosis, intuitive guidance. "No," said the leader, "You are here to be a link between the living and those who have passed over." No argument was possible.

Needless to say, it did not work. But the group ran for several years, the leader was a charismatic figure. There would be rows and members would leave. New members joined, unscreened as to their spiritual or emotional suitability. I observed from a distance, having left rather quickly after a row with the leader. While I did sit with them, I was so well wrapped up that I could pick up nothing clairvoyantly. But it was an invaluable lesson.

It is not always possible to screen groups before they come together. When I lead workshops for outside organizations, I have no way of knowing who will be present. So, while I hold the group energies to contain them and try to create a safe space for everyone, I have to be aware that other things may be needed. It may not always be, according to the purpose of the group, appropriate for it to be altogether harmonious either. A meditation or healing group is very different from a past-life or astrology group, for instance. In the former, the more peaceful the atmosphere, the better. In the latter, people may need a safe space in which to express some highly destructive emotions or experiences. The residue of these then needs transmuting afterwards.

The space where the group takes place may be a sanctuary, kept for that purpose, or a room where a multitude of disparate activities take place. Even in a building used for spiritual purposes, various undesirable entities may have congregated or lost souls have been drawn for help. Certain buildings suffer from geopathic stress, which creates its own problems. To simply open oneself up in such a place for any spiritual activity is asking for trouble. The energies must be cleared and cleansed prior to group use. Crystal Clear essence is a wonderful aid here, a few drops sprayed from a plant spray will clear in minutes.

No amount of prior preparation is going to clear the air if the group bring their own disharmonies with them. Jealousy, envy, power struggles and psychic attack in theory have no place in a spiritual group. But they often thrive there. Strong leadership is called for if this is to be contained and transformed. It may be necessary to restructure the group, or ask a disruptive influence to leave, depending on the purpose of the group. So many spiritual leaders rely on the principle that "love will overcome all." Unfortunately it does not always work, and may not in any case be appropriate depending on what is happening.

Fortunately in shamanic work there has always been an awareness of the "darker" forces and borrowing techniques such as smudging, rattling and drumming can help to clear the energies and release group members from some of the more negative emotional states. As with all spiritual work, however, you need to know what you are doing. Ignorance is the biggest danger in a group be it meditative, occult, shamanic or healing practices that are being followed. The group energy is very powerful, much stronger than its individual parts. This is why, in the past, membership in occult groups was only available to carefully selected and prepared initiates who were under the leadership of an experienced, discerning, and hopefully (although not always) advanced soul. Unfortunately, as the practices have become more widely known, the techniques are available to any power-hungry souls, few of whom have been prepared to spend years getting ready to assume the mantle of power. And, with power being such a seductive force, many charismatic leaders have been able to con, or coerce, their followers for a very long time indeed: a hazard that is increasing daily.

So, the best group protection is to select your group carefully. Choose one that is run by an experienced leader whom you instinctively trust—you will never get far if part of you is holding back through lack of trust. You also need to trust yourself and the other members of the group. This has little to do with personality. You are not required to like all the members of the group, simply to feel in spiritual harmony with them. Indeed, you can learn a great deal from the person you do not like. He, or she, is mirroring back to you what you are most uncomfortable with in yourself. Your worst enemy may turn out to be your best friend in disguise. Choose also a group whose purpose does not inspire fear or dread, one whose basic aims and spiritual orientation corresponds with your own.

You can prepare yourself before you go into a group. Set up the "habit" of leaving your everyday world with its troubles and worries at the door when you attend the group. This helps you to focus on the spiritual purpose of the group and to clear your mind of irritating trivia before you begin. The Bach remedy White Chestnut switches off "mind chatter" so can be a useful aid.

❧ Linking the Group

To forge close links between members of the group, take the FES essence Quaking Grass. Then sit in a circle, linking hands. Picture light passing round the circle through the individual members and the linked hands. (This can be symbolized by the use of an actual rope if necessary.) Ask that the link of light be left in place. (Remember to free members of the group who leave from this link.)

❧ Creating a Safe Space for Group Work

It is the responsibility of the group leader to ensure that the space is ready in advance, but an experienced group may like to prepare it together. Once the visualization has been worked together two or three times, it can become an automatic process that takes place as the members travel to the meeting place. (Visualizations should never be done when driving a car, but putting the thought out that the room be prepared is all that is needed once it becomes automatic.)

Physically, the room can be prepared by smudging, burning a joss stick, spraying with Crystal Clear, placing crystals, lighting a candle, setting up an altar, etc. You can use Indian cymbals or a Tibetan bowl programmed to clear the energies and signal the start of the work. Individual group members can also be smudged.

Psychically the room can be prepared by visualization, prayer, and calling on the guardian beings to be present, in accordance with the group's belief and purpose. Vibrationally, the group can take the FES essence Quaking Grass to blend individual egos and bring about group harmony. A piece of hematite may be placed in the center of the group to enhance trust and like-mindedness (and keep the group grounded!) or another crystal chosen by the group as a symbol of oneness may be used.

❧ Creating Group Protection

Visualize a very bright, white light in the center of the room. Feel its intensity, see its brightness. Let this light grow, gradually expanding until it fills the room. Let it transmute any negative energies it finds.

Ask that the light will direct any lost souls on their journey, and clear the area of any presences not spiritually in tune with the group purpose. The light will act as a psychic broom, sweeping out the room.

Then let the light form a protective barrier over, around and under the room so that only the highest spiritual forces may pass through, unless others are invited.

If the group works with guardian beings, call on them to take their place. Ask that they be present throughout the work. If the group works with a doorkeeper, ask for that presence now.

If you have difficulty visualizing: Feel the energy of the light, its soft warmth and powerful vibrations surrounding you.

⚡ Closing the Group

Let the light build up in the center of the room once again, stretching out a column to each group member. Individually, each person should take what they need in the way of healing, reenergizing or purifying, before wrapping the light around them to form a cloak of protection through which nothing can impinge unless they choose to allow it. They should check that their grounding cord is in place, holding them in incarnation. It may also be necessary to close the chakras down.

Then, as a group, the light should be passed through the room to energize and cleanse it. If a great deal of positive energy, especially healing energy, has been generated, ask that that energy will go out to whomever and wherever it is needed.

If guardian beings have been present, thank them and ask that their protective energies accompany each group member home.

❧ Geopathic Stress ❧

IT IS NOW BECOMING MORE WIDELY RECOGNIZED that the earth energies in which we live affect our physical and psychic bodies. In some places the veils between the worlds are extremely thin: this often correlates with crossing points of earth energy lines (ley lines). In such a place, it is easy to step into another dimension, or for the inhabitants of that dimension to step through into this. The crossing points of ley lines also act as a "fixing medium" for ghostly imprints. This also applies to buildings sited on old sacred sites or burial places. Someone's house may appear to be unlucky: the occupants' lives falling to pieces, or maybe they experience a great deal of trauma; or the house is associated with several deaths. Such houses are invariably sited in places of extreme geopathic stress.

I know of a house which is built on a very powerful earth line between two sacred sites. It also falls in the path of army radar beacons. It is close to a huge burial mound. Several dowsers have confirmed that it was also built on the site of a burial mound—and the spirits were most unhappy about the demolition of the resting place for their bones. The house is in a remote, isolated spot. It had a generator, which picked up the extremely powerful, negative, earth energies and fed them into the house through the electrical circuits. The occupants were physically ill, their lives were a mess, and they were haunted. Any child who slept in the house became highly disturbed. When a dowser who specialized in healing such places went in, he cleared several "lost souls," put in coils to counteract the energies, and found that the people who lived there had had the polarity of their bodies reversed, so he rebalanced these.

However, the energies were so powerful that even these measures were not enough. Eventually, the lines had to be diverted around the house. The only real solution was for the occupants to move to a healthier home.

Some earth energy lines carry positive energy, others negative. There are also a host of other energy lines that can add to geopathic stress: water, electricity, radar, etc. A competent dowser can map these and evaluate the overall effect on a place—and its inhabitants. Dowsers who specialize in healing such places will suggest where to place crystals, stakes, etc., in order to realign the energies. A Feng Shui expert can also be most helpful in such cases.*

Geopathic stress's relevance to psychic protection is that it can adversely affect your health as well as attracting unwelcome guests. If you are depleted and low in physical energy, then you will almost certainly be low in psychic energy. You are then more open to psychic invasion or depletion through psychic vampirism. If you happen to have placed a crystal on a particularly energetic point or a strong line, it will amplify those energies, "good" or "bad."

So, if you feel you may be suffering from geopathic stress, call in the experts. They do not necessarily have to come to your house; many will map or plan dowse, and advise you accordingly. If the energies are particularly powerful or disharmonious, then you may need a visit. It is well worth the cost of a consultation to be free of the effects of geopathic stress.

Vibrationally, you can help yourself with Radiation Essence and Yarrow Special Formula, both of which have been created to counteract geopathic stress. There are also various discs and gadgets on the market which can work in some cases but your best guide here is an expert in the field.

---

* For further reading see William Spear, *Feng Shui Made Easy* (London: Thorsons Publishing Group, 1995).

In Feng Shui terms, even if there is no geopathic stress, the energies created within your house, the smooth flow, or otherwise, of *chi* will affect your well being. Any depletion of the energies of the house will be reflected in your life.

In particular, where you sleep will affect how well you sleep. Beds should not be positioned behind a door as the flow of chi is broken. Neither should you sleep in a position where you can see your self reflected in a mirror. This is believed to disturb the etheric energy and cause insomnia and affect the dream state. It weakens the physical energy and creates disharmonious vibrations in the physical body. So, simply moving your bed and repositioning a mirror may give you protection when you sleep.

❧ Chain Letter Cleansing ❧

WE ARE ALL FAMILIAR WITH LETTERS THAT terrorize us with dire threats, or promise us untold blessings if we send copies to all our friends. The problem with chain letters, even of the "blessing" variety is that we rarely, if ever, know where they come from. If we do, then sending them back to source is the best response. After all, someone who sends a letter threatening our well-being is hardly likely to be someone we wish to remain close to, so we do not need to worry about their reaction. As long as our protection is strong, and we return the letter with blessing energies to neutralize its force, it will not hurt either party. If by any chance it has come from someone you do want to stay close to, then talk about it. Don't let it fester or you will suffer from the consequences. If the letter is a beneficial one, then the sender still needs to know that we do not wish to participate. If I don't know the immediate source, then I send it back to the universe and trust it will take care of it for me.

In recent years a new form of chain letter has emerged—or rather two forms: one promising blessings and good fortune if you pass it on, and the other specifically requesting money. I always dealt with the former by sending it to the universe, and with the latter by returning it as I could not participate. I was receiving up to four of these things a week and, even had I wanted to, it would have cost me a fortune to take part. (I was on everyone's mailing list!)

Then, one day, a letter arrived from an astrologer I much respected. Indeed, all the names on the list were people I knew and respected. The accompanying letter said, "I don't usually do this, but this one is different." There were no threats. You simply sent money to the names on the list. Everyone needed the money for worthwhile projects. This was a time when I was at my lowest ebb. It followed on from the severe psychic attack which had left me without resources, whether energy or money. I wanted to write a book, but needed cash, and time to write. Here was a letter offering me cash, quite a substantial amount of it, for a small outlay. Having money would give me the time to write. How seductive it was. How appropriately timed. It looked as though the universe was smiling on me at last. How I agonized over the decision. Could I break the principle I had followed over thirty years of not responding to chain letters? While I believed that the universe would provide, somehow this seemed "too easy." Even with my bad math I could see how it should work. But, I had doubts. In the end I decided I would send out my twenty copies to a carefully chosen list, and see what the response was. But, if the recipients did not want to respond, then that was it, no substitute names.

Well, I certainly learned a lesson. I antagonized many people, they hated chain letters in whatever form. Other people felt sorry for me and sent me the five dollars but did not want to participate further. Other people were extremely enthusiastic and responded immediately. I received exactly what my outlay had been. Now, I don't know if believing in it more strongly would have made a difference, but in later research, no one I've spoken to who participated in similar letters made a profit either.

Strangely enough, though, since that time I have not received any more letters. The "chain" has been well and truly broken. If only dealing with junk mail could be so easy! (And, yes, I do know about the address you write to but, no, it does not stop!)

❧ Returning a Letter to the Universe

Fire is a powerful purifying agent that can transmute negative energies. The universe is a collective energy that encompasses all. So, returning a letter to the universe via fire cleanses the energy and allows the universe to take care of things for the good of the whole.

You may like to smudge the letter first, or add incense to the fire, but this is not essential. You can either use an open fire or a fireproof container.

Set fire to the letter and watch as the energies are burned and purified. Visualize the letter returning to the universe, to the whole, its ill effects neutralized or its blessing shared with all. Make sure it has completely burned. Scatter any ash to the wind.
NOW FORGET IT! COMPLETELY. FOREVER.

This same process can be used for other letters you wish to cleanse. It is very useful when tie cutting if you find you have old love letters, photographs, or the like, from the person with whom you wish to cut ties. It is not always appropriate to hold onto all our memories in tangible, physical form. The fire releases them.

It can also cleanse the energies where there has been animosity and strife. I once burned sixty proof copies of a book concerning someone with whom I had had great difficulties. It was so satisfying. Every time I poked the fire, there was his face looking up at me— until the flames did their work. Time after time, he dissolved before my eyes. I had been weighed down by the troubles connected with this book. But with every copy that burned, I felt lighter and lighter. And, what is more, it worked. The energies were cleansed. I managed to let go of all my resentment and anger. And things improved dramatically.

❧ Talismans ❧

GO INTO A SOUVENIR SHOP IN GREECE. *You will come out with a small turquoise "eye" to protect you and bring you good luck. Go into a similar shop in Egypt. You will be given a turquoise "scarabi" for the same purpose. If the shop owner takes a fancy to you, you may not even have to make a purchase before the talisman is pressed into your hand. All over Egypt, small boys urge you to buy a scarab, an ancient symbol of eternal life and purveyor of good fortune and health. Talismans or amulets have been used to protect against the "evil" eye and witchcraft since the most ancient of times. They protected and brought good fortune while the owner lived. They ensured a safe passage through to the otherworld after death. Nowadays you can pick up an astrological or esoteric magazine and be spoiled for choice. You can guard against almost everything, or attract whatever you want— if you are willing to pay the price. But, at its simplest level, a talisman can also be a stone you picked up, a piece of wood you happened to like the shape of, whatever takes your fancy.*

A talisman is thought made tangible. Its presence reminds its wearer of the purpose for which it was made, and thus strengthens aims and desires. It prompts you to pay attention, and enhances your intention. As thought is a powerful thing, a talisman can be extremely potent. You can purchase ready-made talismans, but they are most effective when charged to your particular vibration and needs.

A talisman may be a carved jewel: turquoise was a great favorite in the ancient world although in Arabia carnelian was preferred. In ancient Rome, a peridot was worn to guard against enchantment and, set in gold, against night terrors. A talisman can also be a piece of paper with a symbol written on it. The Chinese were particularly fond of this form, red paper being most efficacious. The shaman's pouch is an amulet. So is the Jewish phylactery. The outward form and the material value matter little. It is what is impressed into the talisman that matters. Symbols work because of association and the vibrations set up over the ages.

Many of the symbols found on talismans are universal, having been continuously in use for thousands of years.

Solomon's Seal, for instance, is best known in the modern world as the Jewish Star of David, but it also has connections with India and several other cultures. Its interlaced triangles protect the wearer from evil.

Hands have also been used to ward off the evil eye and witchcraft in many countries. The Hand of Fatimah is still seen on houses throughout the Moslem world: it protects the inhabitants and is also used on vehicles for safe passage.

The Egypt of the Pharaohs was a source of many talismanic symbols. A jewel-carved heart was worn to prevent black magicians from stealing the soul, while the ankh, the symbol of life, gave universal protection. The Goddess Isis was (and still is) a great protective deity.

The buckle that held her girdle was seen as particularly puissant. Usually made of carnelian, it protected the wearer from every kind of evil. There is a wonderful petition to Isis to "enfold me in your wings and protect my days" which accompanies it.

The Utchat Eye, or Eye of Horus was also seen as a powerful safeguard against black magic and was used for strength and courage. It formed part of the ceremonial jewelry worn for its talismanic value, and most of the Pharaohs were buried with at least one around the neck. Tutankhamun—dead and alive—had several about his person.

Both the ankh and the Buckle of Isis passed into the Western world as the Christian cross. Said to exorcise devils and protect against evil spirits, the cross has acquired power by virtue of long usage.

If you wish to make a talisman, it is a simple matter to draw an appropriate symbol on a piece of paper or parchment. Draw it with intent. Concentrate. Ask that it be imbued with the right protective qualities for your needs. You can make the whole matter much more ritualistic, muttering incantations and spells, burning candles, etc. There are many protective amulets and spells in magical tradition. But, it works just as well if you focus your will and have the intent in your heart. When you have the talisman, wear it on your body or keep it close to you.

Alternatively you can purchase a piece of jewelry with the symbol of your choice. If you do this, spend a few moments holding it. Visualize the kind of protection you need: be specific here. Once it is attuned to your vibrations, wear it regularly. Constant use will remind you of its purpose and imbue it with further power.

❧ Flower and Gem Essences ❧

FLOWER ESSENCES ARE "VIBRATIONAL MEDICINE for the 21st century." But they are also one of the most ancient of healing methods. For thousands of years flowers and herbs have been used not only for decoration but also for subtle healing and protection. Garlic was traditionally used to ward off vampires and evil entities. St. John's Wort was strewn with the rushes as a magical herb of protection and burned on the fire to give faith in divine guidance. Pennyroyal was believed to protect against the evil eye. Gem stones too have always been seen as having a protective function: amethyst was believed to protect you from drunkenness amongst other things. Five thousand years ago, the Egyptians gathered the dew from flowers and ground up gems. They used them for medicine, beauty and invulnerability. The Australian Aboriginals used "flower baths," as they still do.

When the young Pharaoh Tutankhamun was buried in Egypt, amulets and talismans were wrapped in his mummy. Protective deities surrounded him, as they did all the Pharaohs. Garlands of flowers were placed around his neck and in the tomb. Several of the plants used related to rebirth and the afterlife. The Blue Lotus which opened its petals during the day, only to close them and sink beneath the Nile at night, was regarded as exceptionally holy because it mimicked birth, death and resurrection. Persea, a perpetually fruiting tree symbolized old and new together. Holy Thorn was also related to rebirth, but it had another function. It helped the soul to emerge from chaos and indecision—useful in the afterlife—and was said to be good for claustrophobia. (Anyone who has been in Tut's tomb will know just how small this is.) Mandrake root, which, in Sumerian herbals of the time, was rubbed into the belly of a woman in labor, may have been there to aid his birth into another dimension.

Maybe in the kindness of their hearts, the priests who buried this young king wanted to ensure a happy afterlife. Or, perhaps they had an ulterior motive. Judging from the horrific injuries to the mummy, there may have been good reason for placating his soul. He could well have been beaten and tortured prior to death. Willow was included to guard against bitterness and resentment, to avoid blaming others, feeling hard done by and carrying a grudge. It gave the ability to make a fresh start and to create a positive reality from one's thoughts. Cornflowers promoted self-love and happiness at being different, protected psychic gifts and, intriguingly, healed the damage caused by institutionalization. Tutankhamun was the Pharaoh who returned Egypt to the worship of the ancient gods. His predecessor, Akhnaten had banished the old gods in favor of the One. His actions had put a great many priests out of business. Naturally, they were understandably annoyed. Was the young Pharaoh Tutankhamun held captive, and maybe even murdered, by the priests, who then decked his body with flowers not only to take him safely into the afterlife but also to prevent his shadow from haunting them? Or was he murdered in a power struggle within the Court, creating an unhappy ka that had to be placated?

We will never know for sure, but we can use the same protective techniques today.

Flower essences are a subtle method of healing which works on a vibrational level. They reach into the outermost parts of the aura, so can work on the physical, emotional, mental and spiritual levels of being and there are essences specially for the chakras. They are non-toxic and gentle in their effect. Many have protective as well as therapeutic applications. They are usually made by steeping the plant or flower in spring water, often under the rays of the sun. They are then bottled in brandy to make stock bottles, which are further diluted in use. The English Bach flower remedies are the original, but there are now many more companies making essences for just about everything under the sun. Applications and dosage differ, but most are diluted down into "dosage bottles;" these contain a few drops of the stock essence in spring water (or in brandy and water to preserve them longer) and then several drops are to be taken two or three times daily. The essences can also be put in your bath water so that you soak them up. The Petal Tone Essences are slightly different. They are applied to the chakras externally, or sprayed around the room. The useful addresses section, at the end of the book, includes suppliers of the remedies, who will provide instructions as to how particular types should be used.

If you wish to heal emotional or other conditions, then a practitioner should be consulted to find what is exactly right for you: remedies are often prescribed in combination and the methods of selecting them vary from muscle testing, or dowsing, to use of a Vega machine. Having said that, there are some remedies which work well for everyone, and several of the companies sell "combination essences" for specific tasks. I have included remedies which I have found effective both for myself and my clients, but there are many other essences which will do the same job.

If you doubt the efficacy and effectiveness of flower essences, Kirlian photography provides graphic evidence. In tests of Vita Florum (a combination of flowers made by Elizabeth Bellhouse), a photograph was taken of a woman's hands. Her energy field was extremely weak. The photograph showed very little light surrounding her hands. A dose of Vita Florum was administered and new photographs taken every minute. Within the first minute, the light was increasing. By the time three minutes were up, the light was brilliant. Her energy field was restored. Other essences are equally effective. If you muscle test for a condition, and the result is weak, a dose of the relevant essence will instantly give a good test result.

Flowers and herbs are also an important ingredient in aromatherapy and the oils can be burned on a special burner during any kind of psychic, spiritual or healing work to enhance relaxation and well being. They can also be placed in the bath, massaged into the skin, or misted into the room for clearing and protection.

The following abbreviations are used in the Flower essences list and throughout the book:

- FES: *Flower Essence Services California (otherwise known as Californian Essences)*
- Bush: *Australian Bush Flower Essences.*
- Gem: *Flower and Gem Remedy Association.*
- Petal: *Petal Tone Essences*
- Himalayan: *Himalayan Flower Enhancers*
- Desert Alchemy: *Desert Alchemy Flower Essences from the Arizona desert*
- Findhorn: *Findhorn Flower Essences*
- Alaskan: *Alaskan Flower and Environment Essences*
- Harebell: *Harebell Remedies*
- LES: *Living Essences of Australia*

Some essences are available from more than one maker, suppliers will advise you. (See useful addresses page 143.)

❧ Protective Flower Essences

For individual use

- **Astral Travel:** *Mouse Eared Chickweed (Harebell)*
- **Aura:** *White Yarrow (Alaskan) Fringed Violet (Bush), Angelsword (Bush), Auric Protection (Gem and Second Aid), Aura Balancing and Strengthening Formula (Himalayan)*

- **Boundaries: Enmeshed:** Wild Grape (Desert Alchemy), **Cutting:** Walnut (Bach), **Lacking:** Centaury (Bach)
- **Calming the Mind:** White Chestnut (Bach), Black Eyed Susan (Bush), Boronia (Bush)
- **Channeling:** Angelsword (Bush), Green Spider Orchid (Bush)
- **Close Down:** Fringed Violet and Flannel Flower (Bush)
- **"Dark Night of the Soul":** Mustard and Sweet Chestnut (Bach), Waratah (Bush), Gateway (Himalayan)
- **Dispersing Thought Forms:** Aura Blue (Petal)
- **Fear:** Dog Rose (Bush), Rock Rose (Bach), Mimulus (Bach), Aspen (Bach), Garlic
- **Fear of Psychic Attack or the Supernatural:** Grey Spider Flower (Bush), Pennyroyal (FES)
- **Forgiveness:** Daggar Hakea (Bush)
- **Grounding:** Sundew (Bush), Corn (FES), Shooting Star (FES, Alaskan), Crowea (Bush), Clematis (Bach), Marizarite (FES), Spirit Ground (Petal), Moss Agate (Gem), Red Lily (Bush)
- **Geopathic Stress:** Radiation Essence (Bush), Yarrow Special Formula (FES), Iug Kenya Energetic Protective Shield (Gem)
- **Inner Guidance:** Mullein (FES), Bush Iris (Bush)
- **Low Self-esteem:** Confid Essence (Bush)
- **Meditation:** Clear Light (Findhorn), Meditation Essence (Bush), Fringed Violet (Bush), Bush Iris (Bush), Red Lily (Bush), Blue Dragon (Himalayan)
- **Mental Clarity:** Cognis Essence (Bush)
- **Nightmares:** Dog Rose
- **OOBE: Safe travel:** Mouse Eared Chickweed, **Realignment:** Crowea (Bush), Sundew (Bush)
- **Psychic Protection:** Fringed Violet (Bush), Angelsword (Bush), Sage (FES), Yarrow (Harebell, Alaskan, FES), St. John's Wort

(Harebell, FES), Vanadinite (Gem), Mountain Penny Royal (FES), Garlic (FES), Red Clover (FES), Auric Protection (Gem), Aura Cleaning (Himalayan), Crystal Clear—in bath (Petal)

- **Psychic Toxicity:** *Chaparral (FES)*
- **Resentment:** *Daggar Hakea (Bush), Holly (Bach), Willow (Bach)*
- **Sabotage:** *Five Corners (Bush)*
- **Self-Loathing:** *Billy Goat Plum (Bush), Crab Apple (Bach)*
- **Shock or Trauma:** *Rescue Remedy (Bach), Emergency Essence (Bush), Vital Spark (Himalayan), First-Aid (Findhorn)*
- **Spiritual Possession:** *Angelsword (Bush)*
- **Space Clearing:** *Crystal Clear (Petal Tone), Sagebrush (FES)*
- **Stuck in the Past:** *Sunshine Wattle (Bush)*
- **Tie Cutting:** *Walnut (Bach) Clear Tone (Petal)*
- **Total Depletion:** *Dynamis (Bush), Life-Force (Findhorn), Straw Flower (LES), Olive (Bach)*
- **Toxic Emotions:** *Holly (Bach), Crab Apple (Bach), Sagebrush (FES)*
- **Visualization:** *Let Go (Himalayan), Boronia (Bush), Bush Iris (Bush)*

In groups

- **Auric Protection:** *Second Aid Auric Protection*
- **Alienation:** *Tall Yellow Top (Bush)*
- **Bombardment by Other People's Feelings:** *Yarrow (Harebell, Alaskan, FES)*
- **Counteract Timidity:** *Mimulus (Bach)*
- **Develop Trust:** *Violet (FES)*
- **Group Harmony:** *Quaking Grass (FES)*
- **Leadership Qualities without Ego:** *Larkspur (FES)*
- **Retain Individuality:** *Golden Rod (FES)*

- *Susceptibility to Others: Walnut (Bach)*
- *Space Clearing: Crystal Clear (Petal Tone)*

Chakras

- **Realigning and Cleansing:** Herkimer Diamond (Gem), Chakra Tonic Formula (Himalayan), Lotus (FES), Bush Iris (Bush), Red Lily (Bush), The Second Aid series of essences
- The Himalayan Flower Enhancers include seven chakras remedies:

  Base: Down to Earth

  Navel: Well-being

  Solar plexus: Strength

  Heart: Ecstasy

  Throat: Authenticity

  Third Eye: Clarity

  Crown: Flight

Recommended Reading

- *Australian Bush Flower Essences*, by Ian White (Forres, Scotland: Findhorn Press, 1993).
- *Flower Remedies Handbook*, by Donna Cunningham (New York: Sterling Publishing, 1992).
- *The Encyclopaedia of Flower Remedies*, by Clare G. Harvey and Amanda Cochrane (London: Thorsons; San Francisco: HarperSanFrancisco, 1995).

❧ Crystals for Protection ❧

TO CHARGE THE CRYSTAL TO YOUR VIBRATION: Hold it for a few moments in your hands and ask that it will perform the specific task. Wear the crystal or place it in an appropriate location.

- **Agates:** *Harmonize body, mind and spirit.*

- **Amber:** *Purifies, draws out negative energies. Cleanses atmosphere of negative vibrations.*

- **Amethyst:** *Provides universal protection.*

- **Aquamarine:** *Alleviates fears and phobias.*

- **Azurite:** *Cleanses and heals. Enhances psychic vision. Opens throat and third eye chakras.*

- **Black Jade:** *Protects against negativity. Enhances wise use of power.*

- **Black Obsidian (Apache Tear):** *Absorbs negative energies. Draws out buried fears. Aids transformation.*

- **Black Tourmaline:** *Deflects negative and psychic energies. Grounds.*

- **Bloodstone:** *Removes emotional and physical blocks. Cleans energy. Cleanses etheric body.*

- **Bogie Stone:** *Grounds and protects.*

- **Carnelian:** *Grounds energy. Focuses mind. Protects.*

- **Celestine:** *Contacts guardian angel.*

- **Flint:** *Aids protection and self-reliance.*

- **Fluorite:** *Shields psychically. Aids astral travel. Brings about oneness.*

- **Hematite:** *Grounds. Focuses. Enhances group trust and like-mindedness.*

- **Jasper:** *Induces deep tranquillity and relaxation.*
- **Jet:** *Shields from negative thoughts.*

- **Lapis Lazuli:** *Heals mentally and spiritually. Removes subconscious blockages through third eye.*

- **Malachite:** *Draws out negativity from self. Clears solar plexus.*
- **Milky Quartz:** *Accesses subconscious mind.*
- **Moldavite:** *Opens higher chakras.*

- **Peridot:** *Heals the healer. Calms. Prevents burnout.*
- **Pyrite:** *Links the brain hemispheres.*

- **Rose Quartz:** *Opens the heart chakra. Brings universal love.*

- **Smoky Quartz:** *Grounds. Draws energy from the crown to the base chakra. Dissolves negative patterns.*
- **Sodalite:** *Awakens the third eye. Clears mental patterns.*

- **Tiger's Eye:** *Protects. Taps inner power.*
- **Tourmaline:** *Provides protective shield.*
- **Turquoise:** *Protects. Aids positive thinking and Oneness.*

❧ Aromatherapy ❧

AROMATHERAPY OILS CAN BE USED TO HEIGHTEN spiritual awareness, increase relaxation, cleanse and open the chakras and
induce a feeling of well-being. Essential oils are highly concentrated and should be diluted before use either into a carrier oil
or water depending on how they are to be applied. They can
also be diffused into the air on a special oil burner or lamp-ring,
or through a spray-mister. A few drops in the bath enhance
emotional well-being and can clear toxic emotional conditions
but the advice of an experienced practitioner should be sought.

- **Angelica:** *Integrates the different levels of being. Aids contact with the angelic realms. Enhances meditation.*

- **Benzoin:** *Balances base and crown chakras. Clears negativity from aura and environment.*

- **Cedarwood:** *Enhances connection to spirit. Grounds.*
- **Chamomile:** *Aids inner peace.*
- **Clary sage:** *Balances mind and emotions.*

- **Eucalyptus:** *Clears negative energy from aura and environment.*

- **Frankincense:** *Invokes faith and inspiration. Balances crown and base chakras. Opens intuition and inner guidance. Promotes stillness. Alleviates nightmares.*

- **Jasmine:** *Opens navel, heart and crown chakras.*
- **Juniper:** *Clears negative energy from aura and environment.*

- **Lavender:** *Opens crown chakra and inner guidance. Clears negativity. Provides psychic first aid.*
- **Lemon:** *Increases vitality. Brings mental clarity.*

- **Marjoram:** *Calms turbulent mind and emotions. Reduces psychic sensitivity, avoiding overload.*
- **Myrrh:** *Opens third eye and crown chakra, strengthens base. Facilities deep meditation. Eases fear.*

- **Neroli:** *Opens the heart. Enhances creativity. Embraces and transforms negative emotions. Reduces fear and shock.*

- **Patchouli:** *Grounds and centers. Strengthens base and navel chakras.*
- **Peppermint:** *Clears negativity from aura and environment. Reduces hysteria and shock.*
- **Pine:** *Clears negativity from aura and environment.*

- **Rose:** *Awakens the heart. Opens navel, heart and crown chakras.*
- **Rosemary:** *Opens third eye.*
- **Rosewood:** *Enhances meditation.*

- **Sandalwood:** *Opens base, navel, heart and crown chakras. Connects to spirit. Quiets mind. Promotes deep meditation.*

- **Vetiver ("Oil of Tranquillity"):** *Opens base chakra, grounds and supports in material world. Aids stillness.*

❧ The Quick Fix ❧

NO MATTER HOW GOOD YOU BECOME AT protecting your self, there will be times when you will need a boost. Certain situations, or people, call for special measures. If you practice these in advance, they will be automatic, and instantaneous. A few are physical but most are simple visualizations. Remember, fear opens the way, so banish the fear.

Bad Vibes, Negative Emotions

- *Fold your arms across your solar plexus, cross your ankles.*
- *Hold up a shield or mirror (physical or visualized).*
- *Jump into a bright, shiny new trashcan and pull down lid.*
- *Carry an Apache Tear (black obsidian) in your pocket.*
- *Play appropriate music.*
- *Stand under a shower.*
- *Smudge yourself with Sagebrush.*
- *Crystallize your aura.*
- *Focus your thoughts on something happy.*
- *Hop into your Green Pyramid.*
- *Auric Protection Essence or Yarrow.*
- *Carry a crystal.*

Dark or Dangerous Places

- *"Make me dim," cloak your light with a black all-enveloping veil.*
- *Call on your guardian or your power animal to accompany you.*
- *Carry your mental sword of protection.*
- *Cross yourself.*

To Ward Off Attack

- *Electrify the outer edges of your aura.*
- *Place a mental mirror in front of the attacker.*
- *Wear a black tourmaline.*
- *Pop the attacker in a bell jar.*
- *Get into your Green Pyramid.*
- *Laugh.*
- *Take Pennyroyal.*
- *If all else fails, try conjuring up a psychic rottweiler or call on Sekhmet (and remember to dissolve the image later).*

Picked Up Something Nasty?

- *Wash your hands.*
- *Shower.*
- *Visualize a shower of light.*
- *Spray with Crystal Clear.*
- *Wear amber.*

Psychic Vampirism

- *Cross your arms and ankles.*
- *Use a psychic laser torch to cut the connection.*
- *Wear a cross.*
- *Carry garlic.*
- *Strengthen your aura.*

Dissolve Thought Forms

- *Use a psychic laser.*
- *Spray with Crystal Clear.*
- *Use a rattle.*

To Protect Your Car

- *Construct a mental pentagram over the car.*

- Ask Mercury for permission to travel the roads.
- "Make the car dim"—wrap it in dark light.

Haunted Place

- Spray with Crystal Clear.
- Visualize light and love pervading the room and dissolving the "ghost."
- Smudge the room.

Lost Soul Hanging Around

- Mentally direct the soul towards helpers on the other side.
- Instruct the lost soul to head for the light.
- Take Red Clover.
- Call in an expert.

Out of the Body

- Anchor your grounding cord deep into the Earth. Reel your self in as though fishing.
- Think your self back.
- Picture your self back in your body.
- Move your body.
- Take Crowea or Sundew.
- Carry a fluorite crystal.

Unwanted Channeling

- Cover your crown chakra.
- Close all your chakras.
- Take Fringed Violet.

To Clear the Air

- Spray with Crystal Clear.
- Smudge.
- Burn a joss stick.

- *Use a Tibetan bowl or symbols.*
- *Use amber or bloodstone.*

"Dark Night of the Soul"

- *Take Warratah every hour.*

Shock or Trauma

- *Take Rescue Remedy or Emergency Essence.*

Auric Protection

- *Take Auric Protection Essence.*

⸙ Common Sense Guidelines

- *Keep your protection up at all times unless absolutely safe.*
- *Know your guide, guardian and doorkeeper.*
- *Know yourself.*
- *Remember drink, or drugs, and psychic work do not mix.*
- *Only work psychically when in the best of physical, mental, emotional and psychic health.*
- *Always come fully back into your body and the present moment after any kind of meditation, healing, channeling, etc.*
- *Remember that like attracts like, work on the highest vibration for the best of motives.*
- *Don't meditate in a place, or in the presence of people with, "bad vibes."'*
- *Choose your group carefully (groups work at the lowest common spiritual denominator).*
- *Don't meddle with what you don't fully understand.*

❧ Visualizations ❧

❧ Basic Relaxation

Lie or sit in a comfortable position. Breathe gently, establishing an even rhythm.

Slowly raise and lower your eyelids ten times. On the tenth time, let your eyelids remain closed. Feel how soft those eyelids are. Let the softness of your eyelids spread out across your face, up through your forehead and over your scalp. Raise your eyebrows, then let them lie gently relaxed. Let the softness move down through your cheeks and jaw. If necessary, clench your jaw, feel the tension, and release. Feel the softness spreading around your eyes, moving to the back of your head. Lift your head and then let it relax back into place. Feel the back of your neck softening and opening, all the tension moving out. Your head and neck are now deeply relaxed.

Raise and lower your shoulders. Then feel the gentle softness moving through them. Give a big sigh and let go. Feel your throat relax. Feel the softness moving down through your chest. Sigh again. Ahh... As you breathe out, let go of any tension that may be left. When you breathe in, feel the softness. Let go around your solar plexus, let the softness move in. Your upper body is now totally relaxed.

Then let the softness move on down through your abdomen. Suck your belly in, then let it all hang out, soft and loose. Clench and unclench your buttocks and let the softness lie there. Let it move down through your thighs and knees. Pull your knees down, then let go and let them lie softly. Let the softness move down through your shins and ankles. Let your feet relax and fall naturally. Your lower body is fully relaxed now.

Your whole body is now soft and relaxed. Feeling light and tension-free. All the parts in harmony and at peace.

Relax and enjoy this peaceful state...

When you are ready, get up and move around. Stamp your feet on the ground to reestablish contact.

⟨ Building Up Energy

Lie on the bed and breathe deeply. With each breath, focus your attention on the point just below your navel. Draw energy into this point as you breathe in. Let it stay there as you breathe out. The point will begin to feel warm and energized. Breathe in energy for as long as you need to feel fully recharged and alive again.

⟨ Guide

Using a meadow or other comfortable place to start, picture yourself walking up to a house on a hill. When you open the door, *your guide will be there to meet you. Spend time with your guide, getting to know each other... (Do not be surprised if your guide turns out to be an animal or bird, or that it can speak to you.)*

When you are ready to leave, ask your guide to accompany you back to your starting point. Leave the house and close the door. Walk back down to the meadow. Before you bring your consciousness back into the room, ask your guide to be available when you need him or her.

Then switch your attention back into the room. Check that your grounding cord and cloak of protection are in place.

Practice calling your guide a few times before you need him or her.

❧ Grounding

Stand with your feet firmly on the earth, a little way apart. You should be comfortably balanced, legs slightly bent if necessary. Be aware of your Earth chakra below your feet. As you breathe in, be aware of your connection with the earth. Feel the breath reaching every part of your physical body, and especially deep down into your belly. As you breathe out, keep your attention focused your belly and on the earth beneath your feet. Make a conscious effort to draw the energy down into the lower part of your body. Imagine you have roots from your feet going deep down into the earth. Keep breathing! Repeat until you feel absolutely centered and balanced within your physical body.

(You can also use this Grounding exercise to let go of negative energy into the earth for cleansing.)

Alternatively:

Picture yourself as a bright orange carrot buried in the earth with just its feathery green leaves above ground. Let your awareness go down into the earth with that carrot. Feel how the earth supports and nourishes the carrot. How warm it is. Feel how the leaves move around in the breeze, but the carrot stays firm and well supported.

Feel how the nutrients of the earth pass into the carrot, bringing it energy and life. Feel the vibrancy of the bright orange color. Enjoy the feeling of being earthed and supported in the ground.

❧ Light Shower

Imagine (image) a shower of light coming down from a point above your head. This light is cleansing and re-energizing. Let the light wash away anything you have picked up that you need to release as the light passes through your aura. Then let the light recharge your aura.

❧ "Make Me Dim"

Take your attention out to the edge of your aura. Pull this aura in towards you. Wrap a cloak of dark light around you so that your inner light is protected and cannot be seen by those around you— and remember to take the cloak off when things are safe again.

(You can also use this to protect your car if you leave it parked in a dark place.)

❧ The Mummy

Picture yourself standing in a cool, shady temple room. In your hand is a large roll of sweetly perfumed bandage. Starting at your feet, wrap this bandage all around your body until you look like an Egyptian mummy. Make sure you cover your head as well. If you need to, leave eye, nose and mouth holes, but ensure that these are protected with light or symbols.

(As a variation, you may like to picture an Egyptian priest wrapping the bandages around you.)

Keep the bandages in place as you switch your attention back into the room.

(You can also use a bandage of light or lead for this exercise, depending on the circumstances.)

❧ Overcoming Fear

Picture your fear as a small furry animal in need of love. Acknowledge its need. Pet it, reassure it, put it somewhere safe and pay attention to it from time to time. Then get on with whatever you need to do.

If you are non-visual: You can concretize this by keeping a stuffed toy with you and petting that.

❧ Psychic Clearing

Settle yourself comfortably in a chair and relax. Picture yourself in a meadow on a warm, sunny day and really let yourself feel the grass underneath your feet and the warm sun on your face. A gentle breeze will keep you cool and comfortable.

Ask to be directed to the right place to do this work. You will need a bonfire, and maybe some running water.

Ask to be shown symbolically all the baggage you are carrying with you that you no longer need. Collect this together in a big pile. Remember to look under rocks, in your body, behind yourself, and other hidden places. Add all your psychic garbage to the pile, all your fears and fantasies. Everything that may be holding you back and making you vulnerable. Gather it all together.

Then look at just how much you have been carrying. Notice how much lighter you feel. See where you have let go of things from your psychical and physical bodies. You may feel some cold breezes blowing through holes, don't worry about this at this stage.

Then find a way to destroy all the rubbish. Throw as much as you can onto the bonfire so that the fire energy can transmute it and free your creative and psychic energy. If necessary, wash or dissolve something in a swiftly flowing stream. If there is a live being that you don't want to burn, put it in a hot air balloon and cut the mooring line. Let it drift away out of your space. Spend as much time as you need disposing of the pile, and really enjoy the feeling of release this brings.

When you have completed the disposal, draw as near to the fire as possible. Let the purified energy flow back to you, healing and sealing all the places where you have let go. Let it reenergize you. If possible, go into the fire so that you can be like the phoenix, reborn from the flames.

As you leave this place, be aware that you are regenerated and reborn, light and pure. Be aware of the energy that flows within you and the possibilities that are open to you.

When you are ready, return your awareness to the room, noticing how much lighter and freer your body feels as you become aware of it again. Check that your cloak of protection is in place. When you are ready, open your eyes.

Psychic laser . . . . *page 40*
Psychic screen . . . . *page 87*
Saboteur . . . . *page 61*

ϟ Shadow

In your imagination, take your self into a comfortable place, somewhere you feel safe and protected. As you explore this place, you will find a pit in one corner. There is a ladder leading down into this pit.

Do not be afraid. Climb down the ladder. In the pit you will meet your shadow. Embrace that shadow.

Spend time with your shadow. Get to know your shadow. Ask what gifts he or she can offer you... You may be surprised at what has been hiding out of your sight all this time.

When it is time to leave, bring the gifts with you as you climb back up the ladder. Thank your shadow and arrange to meet again. Keep in touch.

When you reach your starting point again, breathe a little deeper and bring your attention back into the room once again. Check that your grounding cord and cloak of protection are in place. Get up and move around. Remember those gifts.

The Waterfall

Picture your self walking along a wide valley floor, following a swiftly flowing stream. You are moving upstream and soon the rocky walls begin to rise higher and move in closer to the stream. Ahead of you, you can hear the rushing of a waterfall.

The valley widens out a little to make room for a tranquil pool. Into this pool tumbles the waterfall. You can see rainbows of color glinting in the air above it.

The path takes you round the pool and under the waterfall. Here is a broad rocky ledge on which you can stand and let the waterfall wash over you. Let the water wash away all tension, all emotional debris, all psychic toxicity. Stand under the water for as long as you need...

Then dive into the pool and swim in its tranquil waters...

Then climb out on the grassy bank and let the sun dry off the water.

When you are ready to leave, you will find new clothes waiting for you on the bank. Put them on and then follow the path back to your starting place.

Slowly bring your attention back into the room. Check that your grounding cord is in place. Get up and move around.

Tie cutting . . . . page 99

⸱ Uniting the Elements

Picture yourself standing in a meadow. In front of you is a strong old tree. Go up to the tree and embrace it...

Gradually let yourself become part of the tree. Feel its strength, its living energy. Let your consciousness flow down into the roots of the tree. Feel how the earth supports and nourishes it. How the moisture is drawn into the smallest root hair and then passes up the tree as sap. Feel the warmth and comfort of the earth. Let your awareness move out into that earth, meeting the creatures that live there, feeling the fire at the center of the earth. Draw in its energies....

When you are ready, let yourself move up into the branches of the tree with the sap. Feel the gentle playful breeze moving the leaves. Feel how the small branches whip through the air. Feel the warmth of the sun setting off photosynthesis to nourish the tree...

Then let yourself move out of the tree. You will find that it is raining. Let the rain wash over you. Cleansing and purifying you. You will see a small pool in front of you, get into the water and float there with the rain washing down onto you. Become part of the water, feel its currents, its gentle movements, its hidden power...

As you leave the pool, the sun comes out. Its fiery warmth will dry you quickly. Run around in the sun and absorb its light and energy. Let it revitalize you and give you strength....

Then you will see a rainbow in front of you. It ends at your feet. Step forward into the rainbow. Absorb each of its colors in turn, the red, orange, yellow, green, blue, violet, indigo, purple. Take whatever you need from these colors. Stay with them as long as you like...

Let yourself become part of the rainbow. Feel your self drawn up into the sky. Your feet are on the earth, your head is in the clouds. Reach up to the highest point of the rainbow. Stretch as far as you can over the arch. Then let go, slide over the top, and down the other side. Feel the exhilaration of the air rushing past you...

Let your feet once again connect to the earth, reconnect your grounding cord. Bring your attention back into the room.

ᛤ Useful Addresses ᛣ

ᛣ Flower Essence Suppliers

You may be able to buy flower essences in your local metaphysical bookstore or health food store. If you can't, all or most of the essences can be ordered from the following sources. These stores, in addition to many others, will mix dosage bottles of several remedies for retail customers.

Centergees
2007 Northeast 39
Portland, OR 97212
Phone: 503-284-6603
www.floweressences.com
(They sell over 1,900 different flower and crystal essences, including Crystal Clear.)

Flower Essence Pharmacy
P. O. Box 1147
Sandy, OR 97055
Phone: 1-800-343-8693
Fax: 503-826-1408
www.floweressences.com
(Mail-order flower essences.)

Flower Vision Research
P. O. Box 43627
Upper Montclair, NJ 07043
Phone: 1-800-298-4434
http://flowervr.com

If you are using flower essences in your work with other people and want to order large quantities, or just want to work with the various flower essence companies directly, company addresses follow.

Alaskan Flower Essence
  Project
P. O. Box 1369
Homer, AL 99603-1369
USA
Phone: 907-235-2188
Fax: 907-235-2777
www.alaskanessences.com

Desert Alchemy
P. O. Box 44189
Tucson, AZ 85733
USA
Phone: 520-325-1545
www.desert-alchemy.com

Findhorn Flower Essences
"Mercury"
Findhorn
Forres IV36 0TZ
Scotland
(distributors for many essences)

Flower Essence Services
P. O. Box 1769
Nevada City, CA 95959
USA
Phone: 1-800-548-0075
www.floweressence.com

Pacific Essences
Box 8317
Victoria BC V8W 3R9
Canada
Phone: 250-384-5560
Fax: 250-595-7700
www.pacificessences.com

Pegasus Products
Box 228
Boulder, CO 80306
Phone: 1-800-527-6104
Fax: (970)667-3019
www.pegasusproducts.com

Petal Tone Essences
David Eastoe
Little Lynch
6 Behind Berry
Somerton
Somerset TA11 7PD
England
Phone: 011-44-1458-274-633

❧ Illustrations

If you like the illustration on the cover and want particular illustrations made for you, you may want to contact the artist for a fee schedule.

Judith Page
76 Winchester House
Hallfield
London W2, England

❧ Index ❧